Contents

1

I was born both a witch and an empath. The two are inextricably intertwined as one relies on the other. The empath awareness existed first and the witch reality followed. Now in my Crone years, I feel compelled to share all of this in grimoire fashion so that others experiencing life in a similar manner can know for certain that there's nothing wrong with them, but in fact, everything is right about them.

Grimoires are essentially journals kept by a witch or magician that give an account of beliefs and practices. Many include all sorts of drawings, correspondences, and spells. This one has some of that. But as a solitary witch, I've never had an established tradition to follow so my grimoires have always looked a little different than others

I've seen. And I've always had more than one. I either run out of space, or something happens to it. I had a cat named Furball once who didn't understand he was neutered and sprayed all over anything he could back up against, including my books. I lost so much to that confused fifteen-pound cat.

Although this grimoire isn't a complete reflection of everything I've collected over the years, it does serve as a beginning point for someone who may not want the structure of a coven and may prefer to let the witch in them unfold any way they like. Because at the end of the day, a witch needs no one to define her. Or him. Yes, men are witches as well. However, I will be referring to witches as *she* in this grimoire for readability concerns. It's nothing personal.

I suppose this grimoire reflects a lifetime lived, and while not at its end, I've lived long enough to have a few things to say. I've never belonged to a coven, and I really don't have any interest in joining let alone creating one. I'm certain it's an enjoyable experience, but it's not me. I've always been solitary, but I find many traditions to be fascinating and have incorporated various ideas in my own version of the craft.

The grimoire that follows will consist of two sections: Empath, then Witch. I believe the order is correct in that we begin in awareness (empath) and then manifest form (witch). And with so many empaths in existence now, it's critical that they understand exactly who they are so that they can have far more control and have a happier life.

What many of us don't realize is that each one of us has, and continually uses, the ability to manifest any reality we choose. Because of this fact, empathic awareness is not actually a gift per se, but simply a choice made before incarnating so that we don't lose the awareness of Self. That's it.

Everyone chooses an overall theme before focusing into physical form. Experiencing life as an empath from birth instead of awakening to it later on was simply the choice I made. Not that it's simple, mind you, because it's not. It's that we all possess this awareness. We need only to awaken to that reality.

The seal at the beginning and end of the grimoire is one that I created using the shape of the sun, depicting enlightenment. It includes the words *Sapere Aude* and *Erigo Navitas* at the top and bottom. Dare to be wise and raise energy, two powers befitting a witch, expressing all that I am. In the middle is a bindrune created from both my birth name as well as my witch name. Your witch name should have meaning and define you in some way. You'll feel it when it resonates. Many keep that name secret.

The symbol for Awen is positioned on either side of the bindrune indicating connection with Source Energy. Runes surround the points of the seal, with the Norns at the bottom represented by Hagalaz, Isa, and Nauthiz respectively. Ansuz and Eihwaz represents divinity within and the connection between realms. At the top of the seal, Algiz, Dagaz, and Othala represent Higher Consciousness, Enlightenment, and Sacred Space.

Runes have been a part of my life for as long as I can remember, so including them on the seal felt right. Each one reflects energies of both the empath and the witch and together create a powerful presence.

5

So I hope you enjoy reading the grimoire that follows and that it stimulates creating your own. And as you continue your own thought process about who you are and how you wish to manifest that truth, know that:

We are all truly One in Source.

Empath

It's odd knowing things. My parents assumed I was an eavesdropper. There was no other explanation that made any sense. It wasn't true, but truth such as this evidently was too uncomfortable. To know when bad things are coming is almost too much for a child to bear. And yet I did that every day of my life growing up in an unsafe home. In fact, the only real safety I had was in knowing. At least I wasn't caught unaware, but it wasn't enough.

When an empath grows up unaccepted and unable to communicate with others in a way that validates who they are, life can be incredibly difficult. You have no one who understands you or even knows how to talk to you. It can be such an isolating experience. And when you're a witch on top of everything else, life is never normal.

Some people believe empaths are just people who are overly sensitive. But that's not the whole picture. We're extremely complex and our awareness can be expansive. Because everyone's aura overlaps with everyone else's, empaths tend to pick up the emotions of others. I'll become upset for no reason at all, but it will feel as if the world just ended. And then it's gone. I can't even work up feeling even remotely the same way. That's an example of feeling the emotions of others. I may have simply been in the vicinity of someone who was upset and then began experiencing those same emotions.

Empaths can also be hypersensitive to certain smells, fabrics, textures, or sounds among a myriad of other sensitivities. Dishwashing soaps bother me as do certain perfumes. In fact, most perfumes actually smell like soap to me. It's rare when I find a scent that doesn't.

I went through a period where I couldn't smell bacon or chili cooking. It was so overwhelming and I felt as if it were choking me. When I was ill with rheumatoid arthritis, an autoimmune disease, cigarette smoke made my throat inflame and nearly close over. Now that my RA is under control I don't experience that anymore, but when I did, it was terrifying.

Any boundaries provided us by our physical form do not apply to our nonphysical vibration which is one with everyone else, so it makes a certain amount of sense that an empath would experience other vibrations so intensely. We're experiencing another's focus into form which doesn't stop at birth. It's a continual energetic process. Of course it's powerful and intense. It would be odd if it were not.

Experiencing another's emotional vibration, an empath knows when others are lying and we don't suffer fools as they say. Of course, this applies to witches as well. And we're crushed when we're not believed. But that's how it is when you know things that make others uncomfortable. And it's not easy for empaths to *not* convey what they know. But in the process it can viewed by others as disapproval, even when it's only an awareness of what is. Not everyone wants to disclose everything about themselves. Being around an empath makes that impossible because empathic awareness influences and affects everyone around us.

In close relationships, empaths may be viewed as too intense and may find themselves alone during their lives. That's most unfortunate, but it does happen. Sometimes we're just too much for others to handle, so many empaths become loners. That can also happen because the world is too chaotic for the empath to handle. So we tend to hide out.

In the next section, I will go into more detail about who I believe we all are and how that impacts life as both an empath and a witch. Where we begin matters as does how we proceed while in physical form. Do we become the form we take or do we remain aware of our reality as Source Energy, viewing the body as a vehicle for experience? The choice we make determines our outcome, so we need to make an informed choice.

Where We Begin

I believe that **we're all one in Source Energy** and we only appear separate in physical form. I believe linear time is a construct used to make sense of physical form, but does not exist in the nonphysical realm. With that, our various lifetimes happen simultaneously. It can be thought of as different dimensions, or perhaps viewing our lives after the fact. I also believe that we choose the overall theme of our life here prior to our focus into form. And for me, that theme is as both an empath and a witch.

Additionally, **we never stop being nonphysical beings** while focused into physical form, so ideally we should experience life through that creative lens, otherwise known as remaining aligned with Source.

We are not the bodies we inhabit. We are primarily nonphysical in nature and what we view as physical reality is merely a projection of collective consciousness or thought. It's not for any of us to judge another, but to focus on creating. Remaining aligned with our Source

Energy keeps witches who are also empaths in their magickal presence. We always begin and end there.

We are One in Source, yet **we express ourselves in apparent duality**. That gives the impression that dark/light also means good/evil. There is light, and the absence of light. Anything else is judgment and unnecessary to consider.

We are pure, loving Source Energy; therefore, **there is no dark aspect of Self.** There is only dark aspect of ego. We control our thoughts and our perceptions and see all through Source Vision, understanding that each one of us is here doing the same.

Ours is a constant flow of Source Energy, eternal and everlasting. Stay in that flow and do not become distracted by the projections of others.

We are expressions of Source Energy and consideration of that must be made in all magickal workings. Therefore, **spell work focuses primarily upon enlightenment, healing, and awakening,** instead of binding and curses. A witch arises, and should extend that energy to all. However, should protection be necessary, a measured response is preferred.

It's not up to the empath or witch to control anyone. We're all here for the same purpose. We each play a part in the other's experience. Observe. Align. Know. A witch stands in her own resonance, enfolding others in that loving energy.

A witch holds the balance and the resonance, standing in between physical and nonphysical form. *We're here to observe, influencing only to bring back balance.*

There is *no need for initiation, or for another to define a witch*. She derives her essence from Source, and she alone defines her expression and her way.

At the end of the day, we may be One in Source, but we're not in physical form. Physical form is tricky. Tread lightly.

Pro Tips

Stay in your own lane. Staying aligned in your own Source Energy keeps you out of others' energies. Otherwise, you'll be shielding all day every day.

You attract what you focus upon. Create your *own* reality. Don't participate in another's. Thought is everything.

Everything is a form of energy and energy moves about. Stay in positive energy, moving quickly away from anything negative.

Develop various methods of shielding because not all intrusive energy is the same.

Tunnel method - visualize a tunnel that you walk through, with everything else on the outside of that tunnel. This works great when in big box stores or crowds.

Suit of Armor - visualize any type of protection garment that resonates. With my martial arts background, I prefer anything from a Shield Maiden to a Ninja.

Bubble or Crystal of Light - I prefer the Merkaba as my symbol, with me inside. One actually appears in my natal astrological chart, a grand sextile it's called. Color can be infused into the bubble or crystal, whatever resonates is fine. And if all else fails...

Cast a Circle - It's simplest to find a word that you like, such as *Circulare*, followed by *Erigo Navitas*, or something like that. I happen to like Latin, but words are words. Snap the circle into place, and then go about your business.

Understand that energy vampires exist.

Most people don't mean to be intrusive, but they are nevertheless. They might be needy or just have unhealthy boundaries, but some are invasive with their energy. Gently set boundaries if you can with most, but with true vampires, you **must** shield.

Vampiric energy is sticky. Another method of shielding for those empaths accustomed to dealing with intrusive or vampiric energies, is to align first, visualize your cells as energy, and then move them apart. The idea is for intrusive energy to move through without sticking to you. But this isn't always easy to do for the newly aware empath, so try it and then if it's difficult, use the more conventional approaches. This one takes focus, and vampiric energy is distracting, so do whatever it takes to remain unaffected by it.

Sometimes we can sense the direction of a vampiric attack. Shield or quickly cast a circle. Bring your focus to your still point. Extend your receptive hand and move either deocil (clockwise) or widdershins (counterclockwise) in a circle, feeling the energy coming in. I prefer widdershins because it seems like I can feel discrepancies more easily than when I move deocil. But that's just me. When you sense the change in energy, then you may have found the direction the vampiric energy is coming from. Remember however that it's not always close by.

Additional Characteristics

We are powerful multidimensional metaphysical energy beings. We move best in the in between, in the space between physical and nonphysical form. Try to stay there as much as possible. It's our place of knowing, and our place of oneness with all.

It's common to feel separate from the body. That feeling tells you that you're here to observe. It's the sense that your eyes are not what sees, but that you see *through* your eyes.

The challenge for empaths is to observe, not absorb, the energy around them. What that truly means is that we are the observer, the perceiver of the projection of collective consciousness that we all participate in. Focus too long, we become caught up, and we stop creating. Reaction becomes our process at that point.

The empath knows we are one in Source Energy. But the feeling of separateness which translates into feelings of not belonging or of being different makes life challenging.

Empaths know when other people are lying. Their energy changes. And it's tough not to let on that we know it's happening. Early on, we learn to associate subtle changes with the severity of the lie. Empaths must learn to tell the difference between someone who is guarded and someone who is trying to deceive them, and respect privacy. But for the rest of the people who make things up out of whole cloth, this Crone has no sympathy.

Feeling in is something an empath will do to see what's up with someone or with a situation. It tends to be automatic, and because an empath's focus is so intense, people can feel uncomfortable in our presence. Staying aligned helps in this case so that you don't stay too long in someone else's energy. It's really unnecessary to feel into everything. It's not our business anyway.

Transcend the opinions of others. As an empath, you make others uncomfortable without their even knowing why.

Finding out you're a witch as well typically puts the final nail in the coffin. So stay aligned, away from judgment and see everyone with loving Source Vision. As difficult as that sounds, it's much easier than dealing with all that creative nonsense.

Interaction With Others

I find interaction with others to be both exhilarating and difficult particularly when only nonsense comes out. Although this situation can be described in many ways, I prefer to view it as talking out one's ass. And then I have to decide whether I'm going to call whomever it is out for their lies and machinations. Basically I don't do well around bullshit artists who for some reason all seem to gravitate toward me. Maybe I'm viewed as a challenge.

Boundaries issues are probably the worst part of having empathic awareness. Not everyone possesses healthy boundaries, violating right and left the personal space we all like to have. People tell me their life stories in the checkout line at the grocery store. If I'm ahead of them in line, I might conclude my purchase with them still in the middle of a really long story. At that point, I have to make a decision. Do I offend the person by walking away, or do I try to let them know that they need to wrap up? Either way, I'm more consumed with the fear of offending them in some way than I am about my frozen food melting. I didn't ask for this conversation, but here I am again anyway.

As you can see, taking on the responsibility for someone else's boundary issues is something that an empath needs to avoid completely. This is particularly true when dealing with the more passive-aggressive among us.

Passive-aggressive people are difficult for anyone to interact with. It's as if they stay on the margins, so to speak, without coming into full focus. It typically feels like I'm in the middle of a tornado with all of this chaotic energy swirling around me. I'm trying to avoid being hurt by flying objects (in this case, words) while still trying to understand what's even going on, which I can tell you is nearly impossible.

Honesty in any interaction is vital for an empath. It's our anchor and without it, we're a bit adrift emotionally. A passive-aggressive person is more focused on manipulation and the empath must stay aligned in what she knows to be true, otherwise it's easy to become caught up in the game being played. Have the courage to know what you know to be true. The passive-aggressive person will try to convince you otherwise, which is part of the game. It's vital for the empath to see the manipulation for what it is.

Like many empaths, I have an enveloping aura, drawing in folks with issues like moths to the proverbial flame. As I said previously, interacting with others can be both exhilarating and difficult. Although I always to want to send healing energy to people in distress, experiencing another's emotional imbalances leaves me drained.

At some point, the empath learns to live and let live. We move past the point of needing to balance chaotic energies and let others have whatever experience they want to have. In other words, we stop getting involved. And when we do that, a most lovely peace descends upon us.

You see, it's about allowing, and moving through life in nonresistance. There's nothing earth shattering that needs tending to. We're here to observe and create.

Trust me on this. And try not to wait until your Crone years to make this realization.

And now, for the Witch section.

Witch

This next section discusses how I express myself as a solitary witch and how my empathic nature affects that expression. I have always lived as a witch, although I only *came out* as one a few years ago. I was sure the small wand I wore as a talisman for the last thirty some years would have been a dead give-away as well as the crystals and runes that are everywhere, but apparently not.

I never intended to let this go for so long, but after a point, it seemed strange to bring any of it up. My husband wasn't surprised at my confession and is actually pleased that I finally make sense to him, but I'm not so sure about my tech-oriented boys. Odd, given that scientists, physicists in particular, are among the most spiritual people I've ever known, so why techy people would be any different is beyond me.

Preferring the term Witch or *Wicce* from the Old English, and given my empath nature and my obsession with all things herbal and hedge riding, I identify primarily as a hedge witch. Hedge witches enjoy an *other worldly* experience while expressing their craft. We experience immanence in all things, feeling the collective oneness of everything around us. Riding the hedge is form of shamanic journeying or trance work similar to astral travel and is part of the *other worldly* aspect of the hedge witch. A spiritual practice, hedge riding is when I can go within, away from physical focus and allow whatever truth to be revealed.

I've never been one to develop a personal relationship with this god or that goddess because I view each of them as reflections of Self, but there are a few that resonate. I believe that the gods and goddesses were in all likelihood tribal rulers and/or royalty. Or they were descended from those who seeded this planet. Of them all, Hecate, is my favorite. I'm apparently related to Elen of the Ways, a great-grandmother, as well as Odin. He's a great-grandfather according to my ancestry research. And yes, I believe he existed. I'm just not entirely certain he was completely human. Bran the Blessed is a great-grandfather and his species is listed as a giant, so you never know.

King Solomon (a cousin) as well as various Druid Kings (grandfathers) and the Plantaganet family (everything) are also part of my lineage. Evidently I trace back to Adam and the Blessed Virgin is a cousin. Some of my correspondence material is actually from the Key of Solomon. I began my ancestry research hoping to find witches in my background, which I did, but then to find a great magician as well was profoundly humbling.

I discovered that Lady Janet Douglas, my fourteenth great-grandmother, was burned in the North Berwick witch trials. King James VI is an uncle, the author of *Daemonologie* and the one who recklessly ordered the trials in North Berwick, Scotland. It's unclear that she was actually a witch given the political goings on at the time, but she was burned anyway.

Amongst others imprisoned and/or executed for witchcraft, Queen Eleanor of Aquitaine and Dowager Queen Joan of Navarre, both great-aunts, were imprisoned for witchcraft; Elizabeth, Queen Consort of England, Lady of the Garter, Woodville, my 17th great-grandmother was tried for allegedly using magick to harm Richard III, a great-uncle; Lady Margaret Stanley de Beaufort, another 17th great-grandmother and Henry II's mother, was accused of and tried for the same; and, Lady Margaret Douglas, an aunt was tried for using divination to determine the Queen's lifespan. Francis Stewart, 5th Earl of Bothwell (the slimy one allegedly behind the North Berwick witch trials and who fled instead of facing up to what he did) was a cousin. Family. Goddess help me.

However, as I also believe we were originally seeded here and manipulated genetically by Goddess knows who, I view the Biblical story of creation from a genealogical and historical perspective only. Having said that, knowing the Blessed Virgin is a cousin is cool, but having a magician like King Solomon in my ancestry is even better. However, discovering my Druid heritage took my breath away.

I remember as a child asking endless questions about my ancestors. No one ever mentioned witches or royalty. I had no idea that my obsession with Nova Scotia was due to my Cobequid Planter ancestry. Some of my family settled there as well as in America. John Rolfe, husband to Pocahontas, is my 10th great-grandfather. Many are original settlers in this country, coming over on the Mayflower and other early ships. Thankfully, I've not found anyone in this country who suffered the same fate as my European witch ancestors. Yet.

We choose who we are before we ever focus into form which I believe is a running theme throughout every manifestation. So I feel strongly that I've always been who I am in one form or another. But I have to say that it's odd having family on both sides of the battle so to speak.

With respect to holidays, I prefer to observe the change of seasons that the Sabbats follow instead of the Sabbats themselves, although I do confess to loving Halloween, or Samhain, as it's also called. In fact, it's my all-time favorite holiday. Mabon is nice as is Ostara, representing endings and beginnings for me. I suppose I like what they represent more than the holiday itself. However, I do love Moon, or Esbat, rituals, with the Dark Moon ritual my favorite.

Northern tradition involving runes resonates the most for me, although other traditions feel familiar as well. But my Druid heritage is uppermost in my awareness. I love the stewardship and oneness with the land and nature found in Druid practice. It's something that I've naturally gravitated to all of my life although I've never formally followed that path.

Although I mentioned before that I haven't developed personal relationships with gods or goddesses, I have made an exception with the Disir. Similar to the Norns of Fate, they are three female witches in Spirit who travel together in nonphysical form. Some say they may be female ancestors. They can be accessed in meditation, trance work, or hedge riding. They feel like family to me and I call on them for assistance in ritual and spellwork.

I suppose I'm less concerned however with the past than I am about the present for it's there that alignment with our true Self is found. Traditions and ancestors are wonderful, but in the end, the present moment is all we have.

I think our trouble begins as humans with our tendency to focus on the past. We hang on to things that no longer serve us, keeping us tied to situations that are no longer relevant to the present. This behavior limits our focus and expression as witches, so it's best that we stay focused in the present so that we make the most of our experience here.

Witch as Healer

As witches, we make energy work *for* us instead of absorbing the energy around us. Magick is desire made manifest. Energy is manipulated and directed with intention. Reiki and other healing arts provide a channel for Source Energy to come through, healing both the recipient and the practitioner. This can be performed on a specific individual, or at a distance. Source Energy is All That Is, so it doesn't matter if we're in the same room or in different countries. All are Source Energy, and Source Energy reaches all.

Empathic awareness assists in energy work by aligning the witch with the energy's resonance or vibration so that disturbances in an individual's energy field can be felt. This can present as changes in density, temperature, or vibrational intensity.

Witches who also practice energy work such as Reiki may find they need to shield when offering Reiki. I prefer to cast a circle because entities tend to bother me if I don't.

So, take any precautions you feel you must. It won't adversely affect the healing session.

Chakra crystals can be used in a healing session to further direct and enhance the healing process. Be sure to ground and center before offering Reiki and drink some water or tea when finished to help ground yourself again. The following grounding exercise may be helpful:

> *Begin by taking a few breaths. Feel your breath move in and out easily. Breathe in Source Energy. Breathe out any imbalance you feel.*
>
> *Feel your body sink into the earth, connecting to its resonant energy. Allow earth energies to rise, up through your body and out the top of your head.*
>
> *Feel Source Energy move through you, around you, above and below you, blending with earth energies.*
>
> *And when you're ready, expand your focus, widening that channel until you feel Source Energy flowing into, through, and out of your hands.*

Bring your hands together, and then slightly apart, forming the shape of a ball if you wish. Observe the energy as it moves between your hands. Do you see it, or do you only feel it?

Infuse the energy ball with color, observing its motion. You may see wispy, smoke-like energy, moving away from your fingers as I do. Or you may see something else. It's the same process as observing auras. You may find it helpful to unfocus your eyes a bit in the beginning. You may feel it before you see it, and that's just fine.

When you're ready, begin your energy work.

Whether you're performing Reiki or other magickal workings, you'll want to ground when your work is complete, and this may be done by touching the ground with your hands for a short time. Some folks drink some water or have something to eat. It's important to balance yourself before and after all energy work, whether it's Reiki or magick.

Meditation and Riding the Hedge

I've heard that trance work in the form of hedge riding distinguishes the hedge witch from others. I don't know if that's true or not, but riding the hedge is definitely something a hedge witch does. It's natural for an empath to prefer the *in between* to anywhere else. Truth exists in the in between, in the knowing, and meditation can be used to access that realm between physical and nonphysical presence.

There are many ways to enter that realm using meditative practice. I feel everything, so I can't help but experience the process as a feeling. I begin hedge riding using the same method each time. What follows is an example of using hedge riding to meet with Spirit guides or other entities. This method can be used to begin and end any hedge riding experience.

Visiting with the Disir

The Disir are similar to Norns. Three practitioners of Seidr, or Norse witchcraft. Three witches who feel like grandmothers, and given my background, no doubt are. They guide my way and my love for them is eternal. I use the same process regardless of who I meet, but the cottage is reserved for family. Others I meet by the pond, or somewhere else entirely.

> *After creating sacred space, I begin by allowing myself to pull back from physical presence enough to feel myself melting into all other energy, similar to a candle melting quickly and spreading out on the table below.*

Next, I see my body as separate, my Self hovering next to or just above it, knowing I am so much more than what I see before me.

I turn and see the path I've traveled so many times before, crystalline light illuminating my way. As I make my way down the path, the trees surround me. Ahead sits the grandest tree of all, its roots above and below the ground. It's ancient and it beckons. I climb up onto the large roots, my feet sure. I know my way from here.

The way becomes clear and I move forward, into the root system of the tree, crystal light illuminating my way. Birds sing, and the air is cool. A slight breeze accompanies me on my journey.

The crystal path leads downward into a small clearing. A pond is to the right with stone benches on which to sit. My stone cottage is just ahead, the smell of herbal tea brewing fills the air. The Disir await my arrival and greet me lovingly as the door opens. I am home.

We sit at a table inside, together quietly sipping tea. I am here for whatever they intend. I await their counsel and trust what they tell me. It's a gift like no other.

When the time comes to leave, I take with me the Disir's loving guidance. They walk with me throughout my life, but the time spent at the cottage is a blessing.

I bid the three women, my blessed Disir, my blessed family, goodbye until next we meet. I return along the crystal path, up to the top of the root and back out onto solid ground. I bid farewell to the sacred tree giving me access to the underworld, Hecate's domain, and return to consciousness along the path illuminated with crystal light.

Again, this method can be used for any purpose, to meet guides, angelic beings, family members who have transitioned elsewhere, or for any other purpose the witch determines. I like to simply go there and see what happens or who shows up. You never know what can happen or what you'll experience.

Candle Flame Meditation

Any candle can be used for this meditation although it's nice to consider day, hour, and purpose for supportive energies if appropriate, even if it's white for magicks of increase or black for magicks of decrease.

Settle in and move away from the body as you observe the flame. Focus your attention into the middle of the flame. Allow its center to expand.

Walk through the center of the flame to the other side. Observe. Pay attention to any feelings or sensations you experience. Pay attention to whatever reveals itself.

When you're ready, return through the middle of the flame and back to the present.

Plant Energy Meditation

Settle in and move away from the body as you observe the plant in question.

Hold your hands over the plant, feeling its energy. Allow yourself to merge with the plant's energy, observing and feeling its presence.

Sit with the experience as long as you wish and then gently come back to consciousness.

General Meditation

It's nice to just enter a meditative state without purpose. Pulling back from the body and into Self is also referred to as relaxing into being. You remain aware of everything around you, yet you are separate somehow from all of it.

You may discover as I did that true meditation is in alignment with Source. It's that pure, loving state we enter when we align.

Merging into the surrounding energy feels wonderful to an empath. Stay as long as you like. Rejuvenate. Align.

Meditation seems to be about stillness and emptying one's mind of random thoughts. I've never been able to sit still that long without worrying about how many thoughts entered in. But here's the thing. If physical form is an expression of collective thought, how can we ever not think? So I don't even try to still my thoughts. I'd rather let them go where ever they want. I focus on my breath and eventually I'm able to simply observe whatever thoughts come up without judgment. And I think that's the point anyway, to learn to observe life without judgment. *That* is the true still point, not becoming devoid of thought.

Ritual

The only ritual I perform on a regular basis is drawing down the moon. I've found various invocations that I like and I've settled on a couple that I use for the most part. I won't include them here because they were written by someone else. However, I am including some chants that I use for various purposes in the section on Latin.

Altars are a regular part of a witch's life. I have them everywhere. I typically decorate them according to the purpose involved, so a New Moon altar would have black candles instead of the white ones typically for a Full Moon altar. But a candle is a candle and the witch's intention is all that matters. Use what you have. **You** are the magick.

Various tools used in ritual include wands, athames, censers, cauldrons, the aforementioned candles, a chalice, spheres, incense, and ritual oils to name a few. I try for simplicity and it goes sideways. Every time. I can't help myself. I cram all kinds of stuff on the altar or table. But that's okay. My altar represents my own expression. My mother called it clutter.

In the next two sections, I'll discuss the most important information of all: ritual correspondences. Witches love them. Everything has a vibration and it's nice to find incense, ritual oils and herbs, and smudges that share similar correspondences. It's also useful to blend energies or include them as a counterbalance.

I like to arrange things by day of the week and moon phase. And as with my altar, I can easily overcomplicate the process. The simplest process is to center, focus, visualize and then send your intention. No props necessary. But it's still cool to use the right stone for the right day at the right hour to increase whatever intention you might want to send.

Correspondences

Incense and Resins

Most of the resins I use are from the trees around my home. Fir, pine, and juniper make wonderful resin for burning in a small cauldron or to mix with other herbs and essential oils. Herbal incenses are burned on censer charcoal and are used for purification, protection, cleansing, astral work, or for any intention.

Copal - purification, protection and may be substituted for frankincense

Dragon's Blood

Frankincense

Pine - from my own trees

Fir - from my own trees

Juniper- from my own trees

Myrrh Gum

Benzoin

Ritual Oils

Now in my Crone phase of life, my focus in using ritual oils is on my own spiritual alignment. I never perform spells to derive monetary gain or to influence someone else's outcome other than to help them align. The only real exception might be a binding spell if someone is truly out of control. Spells and rituals are primarily used to keep me aligned in my Source Energy. Anything else is a reflection of ego which is illusion-based. I prefer to stay in my own non-physical essence and proceed from that standpoint and I like my craft to follow that lead.

There are two types of ritual oils that I use: essential and infused. Infused oils I make myself using herbs and carrier oils. I also use essential oils sometimes when making infused oils along with the herbs. But ritual oils are typically essential oils mixed into a carrier oil such as almond or grapeseed. For an earthy type oil, I like to use hemp oil, but it needs to be refrigerated after opening, so I typically make only enough for whatever I'm doing. Ritual oils are for a specific purpose such as astral travel or invoking Goddess energies. There are various witch authors who have written books about making ritual incense and oil and I recommend them highly for correspondences as well as the formulas they include.

Carrier oils can include olive, grapeseed, hemp, almond, apricot, jojoba, and coconut oil. Typically, I use grapeseed and almond because they're lighter. From there I add whatever essential oil(s) I want to use for the spell or ritual I'm involved in. Below are some examples, but you're only limited by your imagination and creativity.

To enhance a spell or ritual for healing, you could create a ritual oil that included cinnamon and sandalwood for example. A love ritual might include lavender and rose ritual oil. Use 1/8 cup carrier oil, or more if you're making a larger batch, and then add the essential oils. The ritual oil can be used for anointing candles or even yourself. Anointing your third eye with an astral travel oil can be helpful for example when hedge riding. A meditation blend can assist the witch in accessing her Higher Self. The uses for ritual oils are as varied as the oil blends themselves.

Oils/herbs I use most frequently by Element:

I like to break everything down by element and work from there. For **Earth** influences I like to use mugwort. Cypress and vetivert are lovely oils to use as well. Mugwort is useful for divination and astral travel or riding the hedge. If you decide to grow it in the garden, give it plenty of room because it gets huge.

The herbs of Elemental **Air** are many and I have several favorites. Lavender, Lemongrass, and Sage are among my most used Air herbs. Marjoram, Lemon Verbena, and Yarrow are also nice. Star Anise may be ground or simply placed on the altar. Lemongrass is used for divination, increasing intuition, and returning to alignment, Yarrow as well for alignment. Sage is for astral travel, smudging, and hedge riding. Lavender and Lemon Verbena are used in purification.

Fire herbs and oils that I love include Frankincense, Cinnamon, Basil, Juniper, and Rosemary. Bay and Sweet Orange are also nice. Peppermint is stimulating and refreshing and Rose Geranium substitutes nicely for actual rose oil which can be expensive to purchase. Cinnamon is wonderful for everything. Frankincense and Basil may be used for purification and protection, while Rosemary is used for healing and alignment. Juniper and Bay are for protection and Sweet Orange is for divination and healing.

Lastly, Elemental **Water** herbs include Chamomile, Eucalyptus, Lemon, Myrrh, Spearmint, Ylang-Ylang, Sandalwood, and Melissa. Jasmine is another and I use that in divination oils. Spearmint and Sandalwood are wonderful for healing and Sandalwood is also good for protection along with Eucalyptus and Myrrh. Chamomile and Melissa are used for purification. Resins I use include Frankincense and Myrrh listed above as well as Pine and Copal for purification and protection.

When using these herbs, oils, and resins for ritual purpose I consider my magickal intention and choose the essential oils, herbs and resins that best support my efforts. If grinding herbs and resins together, consideration is made in the direction of the grinding, *deocil* for magicks of increase and *widdershins* for magicks of decrease. From there I look at the corresponding Elemental influences to see if there's anything else I can add such as a crystal or thorn or something else that might bring additional vibrational support. And always remember that these things are just here for support.

Smudges

My favorite herbs to use for smudges are sage and mugwort. Cedar is nice, but I rarely have any. I shouldo plant a new tree. Mugwort is particularly useful in hedge riding and it goes crazy in the garden if I let it, so I typically have a lot of mugwort on hand. I've seen flowers used when making smudges but I tend not to use them. I'd rather use them in tea. Occasionally I add a sprig of rosemary to the smudge when I want something pungent.

Sometimes I use thread to wrap the herbs into a bundle, other times I use thin hemp cord. Embroidery floss works in a pinch and there are lots of great colors to use. I find my smudges either burn or they don't. It's probably how I pack them together, either too tight or too loose.

Oftentimes I burn sage in a small cauldron on charcoal. I've also made some incense disks that burn nicely on charcoal. Or, you can simply throw some herbs on charcoal. Select herbs based on your intention and appropriate correspondences (day, element, planetary hour, etc), grind them together in your mortar with intention, chanting aloud if you like, and then burn some in the cauldron and either cast the rest to the wind, bury it in the ground, or cast it out over water to release your intention to the collective consciousness. So you get a little spell work in with your smudging. Witches multitask better than anyone.

Crafting Spells

Everything has vibration. Everything. And we try to match complementary vibrations to increase our magickal workings, whatever they may be. So, we might carry some obsidian for protection from negative energy, or create a bindrune for success in a job interview.

In this section, I'm going to include some additional correspondence information that I've found useful over the years. I tend to cobble together information I find along the way into a format that's meaningful to me, so I don't always include information that others might include. As with anything, we can over-correspondence things, so in theory I prefer a minimalist approach. Otherwise, there's too much crap on the altar. I know, because I put it there. But it's good to have goals.

The risk of using someone else's correspondence tables is that some of it may not resonate, so recreating your own is probably the best approach to take. Unless of course you like collecting correspondence tables. Most witches do; I'm no exception. Witches tend to have veritable research libraries at their disposal, tucked in various corners of their home. But at the end of the day, you'll find things you return to again and again, and they'll become part of your grimoire, like these have become part of mine.

Full Moon Names, Sabbats, and Cross-Quarters

There are various groups of people who have given names to the Full Moon. Of them, I typically relate to the Algonquian and Cherokee, followed by the Celtic moon names. I also like some of the Wiccan Full Moon names and sometimes use them when referring to the Full Moon.

There are eight Sabbats or holidays that many pagans and witches observe. Four main holidays and four that are considered cross-quarter holidays, such as the equinoxes.

In *January*, the Algonquians called this moon the Wolf Moon, while the Cherokee and Wiccans refer to January's Full Moon as the Cold Moon. The Celtic people, on the other hand, called it the Quiet Moon. I like the Wolf Moon because it brings to mind a wolf on a cold night howling at the moon, although the Celtic Quiet Moon resonates as well. I don't need reminding that it's cold. Imbolc falls on January 31st signifying the beginning of Spring. Not so on the High Desert. It's also known as the Feast of Brighid.

February's Full Moon is different for each group. The Algonquins called it the Snow Moon, the Celts, the Moon of Ice, the Cherokee, the Bony Moon, and Wicca refers to it as the Quickening Moon. I'm with the Algonquins on this one. It's still cold out and we get snow in February where I live.

In *March*, the season begins to change and the wind picks up, ushering in the beginning of Spring. The Celts and the Cherokee agree on the windy component and call this moon the Moon of Winds and the Windy Moon respectively. Wiccans refer to it aptly as the Storm Moon, and for some reason the Algonquins call it the Worm moon. Maybe that's when worms begin moving in the ground after winter, I don't know. I have three worm farms in my kitchen, so my little guys are moving all the time. Ostara, an equinox, is on March 20th. I typically bury an egg on Ostara to bring fertility in the garden.

April's Full Moon brings signs of Spring and growth. The Celtic people relate this to all things growing and refer to it as the Growing Moon. The Algonquin people call it the Pink Moon and the Cherokee, the Flower Moon. Wiccans are still concerned about wind, so they call it the Wind Moon. As I have some Cherokee ancestry, I relate to the Flower Moon. The 30th of April brings Beltane, the point between the dark and light times of the year. Protection magick can be worked during Beltane.

However, the Algonquins refer to *May's* moon as the Flower moon as do the Wiccans, so sometimes I'm redundant. The Celts call it the Bright Moon and the Cherokee, the Planting Moon. I try to use that one so folks don't look at me funny and ask if I actually know what month it is.

June is a wonderful month and Wiccans call that Full Moon the Sun Moon, the Cherokee, the Green Corn Moon, the Celts, the Moon of Horses, and the Algonquins, the Strawberry Moon. I like that one the best because my strawberries are typically ready to pick during June. Midsummer, or the summer solstice, is the longest day of the year, and falls on June 30th.

Wiccans call *July's* Full Moon, the Blessing Moon. That's so lovely that I can't help but refer to it that way. The Cherokee are still focused on their corn crop during its growth and refer to July's Full Moon as the Ripe Corn Moon. Celtic people call this moon the Moon of Calming, which I love as well. And the Algonquians call it the Buck Moon. Lughnasadh or Lammas as it's also called falls on the 31st and represents harvest.

August begins the time for harvest and the Cherokee and Wiccans use harvest-related names for this Full Moon calling them Fruit Moon and Corn Moon respectively. The Celts call this moon the Dispute Moon and the Algonquins, the Sturgeon Moon. None of them really resonate, so I typically choose the Sturgeon Moon.

Wiccans and Algonquins refer to *September's* moon as the Harvest Moon. The Celts call it the Singing Moon and the Cherokee call it the Nut Moon. I prefer the Harvest Moon because September is typically the time when my heaviest garden harvest comes in. Mabon on the 23rd brings another equinox and represents the end of harvest. I love this time of year, particularly October when I was born.

The Celts and the Cherokee refer to *October's* moon as the Harvest Moon. Maybe if one has a long growing season that name might apply, but I don't have one. I like the Wiccan name, Blood Moon as well as the Hunter's Moon from the Algonquins. Blessed Samhain, or Halloween as it's usually called, is the time when the veil is thinnest and we have the best access to ancestors who have already passed over. As everyone knows, it occurs on the 31st, and for some it represents the end of the year and the beginning of the new one. It is my favorite holiday. Christmas has nothing on Halloween. My decorations are a permanent fixture.

The Algonquin's refer to **November**'s full moon as the Beaver Moon. Celtic people called this moon the Dark Moon. Wiccans named it the Mourning Moon, and the Cherokee called it the Trading Moon. I prefer the Celtic name to the others.

December's full moon is called the Cold Moon by both the Celts and the Algonquian. The Cherokee refer to it as the Snow Moon and Wiccans call it the Long Night's Moon. I like them all, but the Long Night's Moon reminds me of the story of Santa Claus and it's my favorite. Yule occurs on the 21st and is known as the winter solstice.

Correspondences by Day

There are lots of tables around in various compilations. Some are interesting to me and some aren't particularly relevant. I like to break things down by both the phase of the moon and the day of the week. From there, I can add the appropriate crystal, or choose the right candle color. My favorite correspondences are below and they reflect the considerations I make when practicing my craft. Unless I wing it.

Sunday – The Sun rules Sunday and represents Elemental Fire. Its direction is South and its energy is Masculine or Projective in nature. Aries, Leo, and Sagittarius are Sunday's astrological correspondences. Sunday's colors include yellow, orange, and gold.

Resins for Sunday include frankincense, myrrh, and dragon's blood. Basil, cinnamon, garlic, and juniper are its herbs.

The Sun expresses the witch's power, *to will,* and can be useful during the moon's waxing phase for magickal workings for employment and friendship concerns. During the waning phase, the Sun's influence is helpful in removing barriers, preventing war, and locating something that's been lost.

Runes include Thurisaz, Kenaz, Nauthiz, Sowilo, and Inguz. Tarot correspondences include Wands, Swords in some perspectives, The Sun, Strength, and the Emperor.

Monday – Moon is Monday's ruler and represents Elemental Water. Its direction is West and its energy is Feminine or receptive. Cancer, Scorpio, and Pisces are the astrological correspondences and its colors are white and silver, and I might include some selenite or moonstone on the altar. Pearl is nice as well.

Lunar herbs include mugwort, yarrow, hyssop and olive is among Monday's tree correspondences. Resins and incense include sandalwood, camphor, and amber.

To dare is the witch's power expressed by Monday's influences. During the moon's waxing phase, magickal workings on behalf of feminine balance and healing are recommended; during the waning phase, divination and hedge riding are performed.

Runes include Uruz, Gebo, Hagalaz, Isa, Perthro, Ehwaz, Laguz, and Dagaz, while Tarot correspondences for Monday include the suit of Cups, the Moon, Death, and the Lovers.

Tuesday – Mars, from the Fire Element correspondence, is Tuesday's ruler. Masculine or projective energy, a Southern direction, and Aires, Leo, and Sagittarius are Tuesday's astrological correspondences.

Red candles and stones are useful on the altar along with bloodstone, loadstone, and amethyst. I might also include Herkimer diamond.

Herbs of Mars include cinnamon, absinthe, rue, garlic, nettle, and onion, while trees include thorn, juniper, and dogwood.

Tuesday shares its magickal power *to will* with the Sun with the focus of magickal workings on banishing, purification, and protection.

Rune and Tarot correspondences for Tuesday are the same as for Sunday.

Wednesday – Mercury and Elemental Air influence Wednesday, with Gemini, Libra, and Aquarius its astrological signs and East its direction.

Emerald, agate, fluorite, and topaz are among the stones that can be used on the altar along with green candles.

Herbs and resins for Wednesday include marjoram, cinnamon, cinquefoil, lavender, benzoin, and frankincense.

To know is the magickal focus of Wednesday. With Mercury's Air element influence, magickal workings center on education, study, and divination. Healing and improving communication under the moon's waxing influence, and banishing illness and poor communication.

Thursday – Jupiter is Thursday's ruler, an Air Element, although some say Earth, Water or Fire, which makes assigning planets an interesting process, although typically its Taurus, Virgo, and Capricorn. I've always considered Jupiter an Earth element, perhaps because of its size. It feels heavy to me. But others consider Jupiter to have Air qualities. Jupiter also feels like the balance point between inner and outer planetary influences.

In any event, Jupiter's color is blue and its stones include jasper, sapphire, and emerald.

Herbs include basil, mints, elecampane, bugloss, and henbane; poplar, oak, plum, apple, olive, and fig are Thursday's trees. Resins and incense include balm, ambergris, and saffron.

Jupiter's magickal power could be any of the four, but given its expansiveness, either the influence of Earth or Air would be appropriate to consider. Although *to know* aligns with Air, and *to keep silence* with Earth, it could also apply to Air, and I view this as Jupiter's resonant influence.

Prosperity, protection, grounding, and ancestor oriented magickal workings are influenced by Jupiter's expansive energy. Runes include Fehu, Wunjo, Jera, Berkano, Mannaz, and Othala; Tarot correspondences include the suit of Pentacles, the Devil, Empress, Emperor, and the World.

Friday – Venus is Friday's ruler and shares both Air and Water elemental influences and has feminine or receptive energy. Its astrological correspondences include Cancer, Scorpio, and Pisces and the direction is typically West.

Its color is green and its stones include rose quartz, lapis, carnelian, and turquoise. Vervain, rose, violet, valerian, and thyme are among Friday's herbs. Incenses include sandalwood and ambergris.

The magickal power of *to dare* is shared with Monday with an emphasis on magickal workings centering on love, friendship, and beauty. Divination, healing, and fertility are also appropriate here.

Uruz, Gebo, Hagalaz, Isa, Perthro, Ehwaz, Laguz, and Dagas are Friday's runic correspondences, while the suit of Cups, the Moon, Death, and Lovers are its tarot cards.

Saturday – Saturn is the planetary ruler of Saturday and its Element is Earth. Its direction is North, and has feminine or receptive energy. Taurus, Virgo, and Capricorn are Saturday's astrological correspondences, and black is its color.

Stones include onyx, jet, jade, emerald, and sapphire. I also like smoky quartz. Herbs and resins include cypress, rue, dragonwort, benzoin, and cumin.

To keep silence is the magickal power associated with Saturday's earthy influence. Magickal workings concerning home, purification, and harvest are useful on Saturday.

Runic correspondences include Fehu, Wunjo, Jera, Berkano, Mannaz, and Othala. Tarot correspondences are the suit of Pentacles, the Devil, Empress, Emperor, and the World.

Planetary Hours

Witches try to cast spells when energies align. Observing moon phase or planet position can either support or detract from a spell's success. For the most effective use of planetary information, we need to know what planet governs what hour and since sunrise and sunset occur at different times each day, we need to know that information as well. From there, we can create our own table as a diagram to assist in performing a spell at the best time. Yes, it involves math. We can use an existing table to determine which hour belongs to which planet or we can figure it out ourselves, but we still need to do the math to know when each hour begins and ends. Sorry.

Also, in the *Key of Solomon* there's something called the Chaldeon Order of planets: Saturn, Jupiter, Mars, Sun, Venus, Mercury, and the Moon. It repeats, and it's the order we'll use when creating our tables. We know from the Day Correspondence section that planetary rulers are also assigned to a particular day of the week and these will begin each day's column. From there, the column is filled in according to the Chaldeon Order. Sunday's ruler is the Sun, Monday - the Moon, Tuesday - Mars, Wednesday - Mercury, Thursday - Jupiter, Friday - Venus, and Saturday - Saturn. We can create a table by knowing the day on which the spell will be performed, inserting the exact times from all that exciting math we'll do to then know what hour to choose that best reflects the planetary influence we want to use.

1. Determine when the sun rises and sets for the day in question. Go here to find that out. Otherwise, copy and paste the following in your browser. http://aa.usno.navy.mil/data/docs/RS_OneDay.html
2. Figure out how many daylight minutes between those two times
3. Divide daylight minutes by 12
4. Create your daylight hours table from there. If the number from dividing by 12 equals for example, 58, and sunrise is at 6:30am, then we'd begin our first planetary hour at 6:30am and end the hour at 7:28am and so forth

Now for the nighttime hours:

1. Refer to the information you gathered on the time of sunset, and then look up when the sun rises on the following day

2. Yep. Do the math again to determine how many minutes between the two
3. Again, divide that figure by 12
4. Using the same method above, create your nighttime table

You should as an exercise create your own lookup tables as planetary reference to save time in the future. You can then copy down the day column needed, using the methods described above to calculate the exact times of each hour.

I prefer to keep things as simple as possible. Given that a witch *is* magick, we really don't need anything to effectively cast a spell, but it is nice to get as much energetic support as possible. That's why many witches use any number of support tools in ritual or spellcasting. The more aligned energies the better and everything has a vibration. Like or complementary vibrations increase a spell's intensity, so use what resonates. It's also interesting to use differing vibrations to balance or reverse something, such as using the rune, *Isa*, to stop unwanted behavior.

Following is a planetary hours table I've created as an example.

Planetary Hours Table

AM	Sun	Mon	Tue	Wed	Thur	Fri	Sat
1	Sun	Moon	Mars	Merc	Jup	Ven	Sat
2	Ven	Sat	Sun	Moon	Mars	Merc	Jup
3	Merc	Jup	Ven	Sat	Sun	Moon	Mars
4	Moon	Mars	Merc	Jup	Ven	Sat	Sun
5	Sat	Sun	Moon	Mars	Merc	Jup	Ven
6	Jup	Ven	Sat	Sun	Moon	Mars	Merc
7	Mars	Merc	Jup	Ven	Sat	Sun	Moon
8	Sun	Moon	Mars	Merc	Jup	Ven	Sat
9	Ven	Sat	Sun	Moon	Mars	Merc	Jup
10	Merc	Jup	Ven	Sat	Sun	Moon	Mars
11	Moon	Mars	Merc	Jup	Ven	Sat	Sun
12	Sat	Sun	Moon	Mars	Merc	Jup	Ven

PM	Sun	Mon	Tue	Wed	Thur	Fri	Sat
13	Jup	Ven	Sat	Sun	Moon	Mars	Merc
14	Mars	Merc	Jup	Venus	Sat	Sun	Moon
15	Sun	Moon	Mars	Merc	Jup	Ven	Sat
16	Ven	Saturn	Sun	Moon	Mars	Merc	Jup
17	Merc	Jup	Ven	Sat	Sun	Moon	Mars
18	Moon	Mars	Merc	Jup	Ven	Sat	Sun
19	Sat	Sun	Moon	Mars	Merc	Jup	Ven
20	Jup	Ven	Sat	Sun	Moon	Mars	Merc
21	Mars	Merc	Jup	Ven	Sat	Sun	Moon
22	Sun	Moon	Mars	Merc	Jup	Ven	Sat
23	Ven	Sat	Sun	Moon	Mars	Merc	Jup
24	Merc	Jup	Ven	Sat	Sun	Moon	Mars

Knot Magick

There's a myriad of ways to perform magick, but I really like using knot spells. I prefer soft leather to anything else, otherwise I use hemp cord that's been braided to create a cord of more substance. The number of cords I use ranges from one for something simple to more if I need to influence something more complex, weaving each together with the other cords. A simple knot can be used or something more complex. I prefer using figure eight knots unless I really need to focus, in which case I tie more complicated knots. The casting can be carried on your person as a talisman or charm. Or it can be burned or buried if the working requires it.

There are many versions of the chant that's recited while tying the knots. A witch can use any order or pattern she likes as well as the type of knot she uses. Knot spells can be worked at any time but they have special significance and power for me if performed when the Moon is either Dark or Full. Each separate moon phase has its own energy, but I only break it down to waxing or waning moon phase. As with any spell, correspondences regarding day, hour, and time should be observed whenever possible as well as any other correspondences that are appropriate. Specific colors may be selected to also enhance the casting.

The words spoken

There are various renditions of the basic knot spell. The idea is, if you borrow another witch's written spell, modify it to make it your own. This is the one I use.

With the knot of one, my spell has begun
With the knot of two, my spell is blessed true
With the knot of three, my power flows free
With the knot of four, my intention is stored
With the knot of five, energy rising and alive
With the knot of six, my intention fixed
With the knot of seven, the spell has leavened

With the knot of eight, coalesce into fate

With the knot of nine, my desire, mine

Order matters, or not

---1-----6-----4------7-----3------8-----5-----9-----2---

Some witches use an order when tying knots. But if you don't want to do that, you don't have to. Some knot magick uses the typical 9 knots, but I also perform one that uses 13. Really, any number can be used because it's all about the witch's magickal will and intention.

Number correspondences can also be used when choosing the number of knots used. If the magickal working was to increase stability or security, then six knots could be used for example.

Knot magick can be used during Dark Moon ritual to set intentions for the Full Moon and untied at that time. That's the best aspect of knot magick. You can truly make it your own. Adding beads or shells or other objects that have significance can also be part of the casting. It's really all up to the witch how she uses knot magick in her craft. Above is the typical 9-knot order to use if you like.

So if you haven't worked knot magick, give it a try! It might become your favorite magickal tool. Witches who are skilled at macrame should have no problem. For the rest of us, I recommend starting with a simple knot or maybe the figure 8. Your focus needs to be on your intention instead of getting the knots right. If you have to refer to a diagram, it breaks your focus, so work the knot until you're comfortable tying it without thinking about it. And if you don't happen to have your cords with you when you feel the need for some knot magick, don't worry. You can visualize the cord(s) as well as the knots as they're tied. Above all, have fun with it!

Rune Magick, Sigils, and Magic Squares

Full disclosure: I'm a symbol junkie. I love them. Symbols, or sigils, may be used when crafting spells and rituals. Sigils can be made using magic squares and bindrunes can be created from combining various runes together. From there, the sigil or bindrune can be utilized during ritual, carried as a talisman, or drawn as a sign of some kind as in the case of hex symbols. Bindrunes are also used for the purpose of rune magick.

Bindrunes

I dearly love bindrunes. Each rune in the Futhark has vibrational resonance, and when combined together in a meaningful fashion, that resonance can be directed and increased. Protective power of some kind is a common theme, as is balance and immanence. We're all extensions of Source Energy. It's our essence that has no beginning and no end. Our natural state is a blending of energies in Oneness and runes point the way to that remembrance. As the vibrational frequency of Gaia rises, understanding this truth is critical. Our focus must now be in raising our collective energy, our collective vibration. Symbols such as bindrunes assist in that focus making bindrunes a powerful form of magick.

When creating bindrunes, I begin with a purpose and then select runes that might be helpful. In this example, I wanted to create a focus or talisman for clarity when interacting with guarded or manipulative people. I chose Hagalaz, Sowilo, and Kenaz for just that purpose. Hagalaz, the witch rune, provides the structure for this bindrune while Kenaz and Sowilo provide the energies for illumination and clarity.

As an empath, I know things. Awareness comes like a memory would, it's just there without having to work for it. An empath *feels in* and is then able to get general impressions about what's going on. From there, it's not uncommon for the empath to get more specific details, giving her a more complete picture.

Typically I like to let awareness come to me without wanting to influence that process. But when I'm dealing with someone who is extremely guarded, or who outright lies, then I might need a bindrune as a focus so that I'm not distracted by whatever manipulation is happening. I find manipulation outrageous, and I tend to want to *get into it* with people who do it, if only to convince them to stop.

Another purpose for a bindrune like this one would be to influence the energies of a particular moment, in this case, to encourage honesty. Empaths and witches detest liars. They're pathetic to begin with and we always know it's happening, so why anyone interacts that way with us is

beyond me, but they do it anyway. A bindrune to
hold during the interaction makes it more likely that I'll
get to the bottom of whatever nonsense is going on. Not
that it makes any difference, mind you, because most folks
who lie aren't interested in telling the truth anyway, but at
least I know what's actually happening. And that's better
than the alternative.

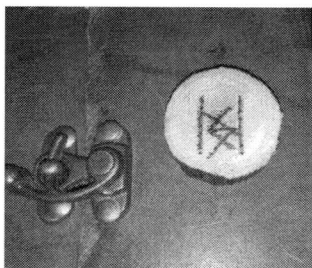

So in the making of the bindrune, I write out each rune
that I'm going to use and then choose which one to use as
a beginning point. In this case I chose Hagalaz. From there
I drew Sowilo and then Kenaz.

Hagalaz begins the structure or framework for the rune
magick. Sowilo brings illumination and Higher Self
awareness to the witch. Kenaz, the rune of openings

symbolized by the torch, represents *to know*, one of the four powers of the witch, and strengthens the witch's intuition. With a bindrune such as this, the witch can remain aligned and undistracted as she knows the truth.

Bindrunes can be drawn on paper or on anything really. I like to use a wood burner and burn them on various pieces I've gathered from trees around my property. I also like drawing them in earth or sand, or carving them into candles for ritual. Protection bindrunes, or hexes as they're sometimes called, are often found painted on barns and homes. A witch can also draw them in the air with her finger, hand, wand, or athame, intoning each rune comprising the bindrune.

This bindrune can be carried or worn to bring clarity and truth to the interaction. The witch may also find the bindrune helpful in remaining unaffected by the goings on around her. Not everything requires a response. Sometimes it's enough to simply observe...and know.

Protection Bindrunes

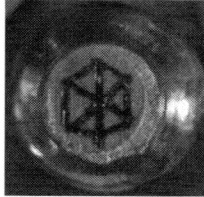

Shielding

A shielding bindrune is used to protect the individual from the energy that naturally flows from others. Empaths in particular find carrying some sort of talisman helps shield themselves from energy that's vampiric in nature. Crystals are also great to carry as well. I carry both. This bindrune is comprised of Uruz (Strength), Algiz (Protection), Berkano (Purity), Thurisaz (Protection), Dagaz (Clarity), and Tiwaz (Warrior). Yes, I got carried away. Typically, unless you're creating a person's name in a bindrune, you would use three at most. But it depends upon the need, and that day I was feeling inundated and overwhelmed by others' energies so it ended up resembling a shield.

Protection from Vampiric Energy

Next up, a more specific bindrune for dealing with vampiric energy. Sometimes we find that others are drawn to us and we're always listening to someone's issue or relationship problem, or whatever else they might want to share. Total strangers will tell me the most personal stories, you know, in the check outline at the grocery store, in the waiting room of the doctor's office, pretty much anywhere really. That's what happens when one is an empath. If you don't like it, then don't go around people.

The type of vampiric energy that this bindrune deals with is more direct vampiric energy, intentional in nature and extraordinarily uncomfortable. Created from Sowilo (Victory), Algiz (Protection) and Eihwaz (Defense), this bindrune brings all elemental energies together, specifically targeting the boundary issues these people seem to have, protecting the wearer from unwanted attacks. Through Eihwaz, it invokes and preserves the wearer's spiritual alignment, reinforced by Algiz, the rune of Higher Power. Sowilo, the rune of Light, Energy and Revelation increases the effect, binding all three together in victory. It speaks to the fact that as we stay in alignment with Source, we "need do nothing" as *A Course in Miracles* would say. This bindrune serves as that reminder.

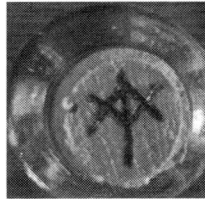

Binding Negative Behavior

Binding Negative Behavior is a bindrune used both in spellwork, and for carrying on one's person, when it's necessary to bind someone's negative behavior from affecting you anymore. It sits on the altar during a binding ritual, increasing the effectiveness of that ritual. It can then be carried in the pocket when around the person in question as a protection talisman. Created from Tiwaz (Warrior) and Algiz (Protection), and symbolizes our elemental connection between Earth and Spirit. The energy flows toward Source, assisting the witch in remaining in alignment and resonance, where nothing of this world can enter.

Balancing Bindrunes

Healthy Communication

Thurisaz breathes new life into the relationship with its blending with Raidho (Inner Journey) and Laguz (Water). Encouraging healthy communication is the focus of this positive bindrune. Instead of protection, it indicates going with the flow, while Thurisaz suggests that we let go of what no longer serves us. Raidho allows a change in our thinking as we co-create better relationships together. New beginnings are ahead!

Healing

With Healing, we address the balance it takes to remain healthy. Tiwaz (Warrior), promising quick recuperation, gives us the impetus or warrior spirit to heal whatever befalls us, whether physical, emotional or spiritual in nature. Dagaz (Clarity, New Day) instructs us transformation back to health is possible as we achieve balance. Useful in healing ritual work, this healing bindrune focuses Divine energy, infusing healing potential into energy raised and projected.

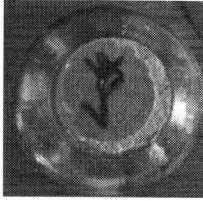

Balance

Lastly, this Balance bindrune joins Algiz (Higher Power) with Wunjo (Harmony) and Eihwaz (Defense). Wunjo is the balancer between Algiz and Eihwaz, blending both one's Higher Self with the physical body's natural need for self-defense. Wunjo is also the rune of the Law of Attraction. As we attract the energy we focus upon (doesn't matter if it's good or bad), Wunjo brings harmony and joy to the situation so that we view it with the clarity that alignment with Source brings.

Essentially, Wunjo is the balance between the two polarities that allows the individual to see through the eyes of Source, drawing upon the inner, more expansive Spirit to provide the clarity to see that we *need do nothing*. Perception gives way as we stand in our own truth.

Immanence Bindrunes

We are One with Source. We are not the bodies that seem to exist. We are Spirit, in Oneness with All That Is. A piece of our attention is here, focused into a physical existence, while the remaining, more expansive piece exists blended together in Oneness. Bindrunes reflecting this immanence serve not only as a focus for this awareness, but also as a reminder of who we actually are.

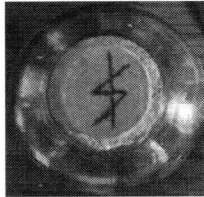

Source Energy

Source Energy blends Sowilo with Fehu. Sowilo, the rune of Light, Energy and Revelation combines with Fehu, the rune of Wealth to illustrate that our true wealth lies in our extension as Source Energy. As the *sending* rune, Fehu speaks to who we are as we incarnate into this life, with

Sowilo providing the clarity that lights our way as we extend abundance and love as we follow our soul's path.

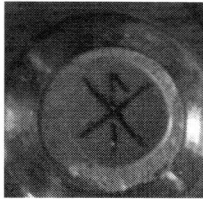

Alignment with Source

As we go forward in life, Gebo and Laguz are used in this bindrune depicting Alignment with Source. Gebo is the rune of balanced energy exchange, while Laguz encourages us to go with the flow. This bindrune focuses us into the now, the present moment, where alignment happens. We're not distracted by anything that is not of Source. Past and future are of the ego and remaining in alignment with Source keeps us moving forward in a positive direction.

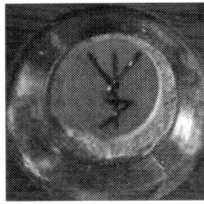

Higher Power

Engaging with our Higher Power is the focus of this bindrune. Sowilo and Algiz are joined to increase awareness of our Higher Self, allowing that connection with Source to flow through us as we engage with the physical world.

Allowing

Along with the Higher Power bindrune, Allowing reminds us that resistance is of the ego and of the physical world, and when acting through our Higher Self it allows us to perceive without judgment, instead moving around whatever doesn't resonate with our Higher Self. Alignment with our Higher Self brings into resonance the Oneness with others through the joining of Laguz and Dagaz, that we could be feeling, instead of focusing upon ego related responses that foster resistance. Staying in the flow, Laguz, of one's Higher Power is true Allowing. Dagaz reveals that only truth surrounding the ego is hidden, whereas all truth is revealed in alignment with Source. Drop resistance and simply allow..

Divinity

Sowilo, Ansuz, Eihwaz, and Algiz were blended to represent Divinity. Source Energy, Protection, Higher Power, Life Force all comprise our Immanence with the Divine. With the addition of Ansuz, we have the blending of Divine Wisdom into the other attributes, bringing further balance to the energies.

As Above So Below

I love that expression, as above so below. It says everything about our experience here in this life. We are to express ourselves while here as extensions of Source Energy. We become confused about that as children when we're shaped by the world around us, becoming more and more reactive to whatever is happening at the moment. Eventually we're so immersed in all that drama that we become victims of our self-created illusions. This bindrune helps us remember that our true essence is one of Spirit and that all the loving energy emanating from Source should emanate from us as we progress through our lifetimes here. Loving intention would be another name for this bindrune.

Magick Circles

Sigils can be drawn using a magick square or circle of some kind, or drawn free-hand. When using a magick circle, one method is to arrange the letters of the alphabet in a circle, and then place another piece of paper on top where the letters of the word or name are traced, creating a design. Or you can simply look at the circle as a guide and draw your sigil free hand. You can also create a magick circle using the numbers one through nine.

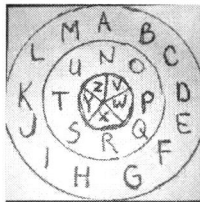

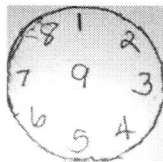

Magick Squares

Various planetary-oriented magic squares are available for use that require numerological conversion of whatever you're using. So if you used the word *witch* then you'd use the numerology table to find the numerological equivalent of each letter and then trace the sigil using those numbers and whichever planetary table that supports your intention.

1	2	3
4	5	6
7	8	9

The simple square above is a table that uses the numbers one through nine. I reduce whatever I'm using to its lowest form, eliminating any duplicate letters and then I begin to draw the table. Referring to the numerology table below, and again using the word *witch*, you derive 5, 9, 2, 3, and 8. No numbers repeat, so you'll use each one. Begin at five and draw a straight line to 9, then 2, then 3, finishing with 8.

1	2	3	4	5	6	7	8	9
A	B	C	D	E	F	G	H	I
J	K	L	M	N	O	P	Q	R
S	T	U	V	W	X	Y	Z	

Below are examples of sigils created from both a magick circle and square. The sigil can be drawn in the air or on the surface of your choice in ritual or magickal workings. It can also be carved or otherwise drawn on something that can be carried as a talisman. The witch decides its purpose. But you can surely see that the shape of the sigil changes depending upon the circle or square used. You can create your own as well.

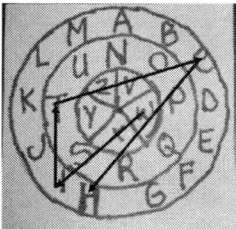

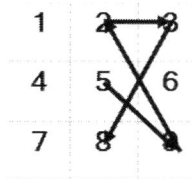

A Few Spells and Some Latin

I like writing my spells and rituals in Latin. I'm not fluent, mind you, but I've had two years of high school Spanish and two years of college French, so with some Latin dictionaries, translation software, and an online Latin course, I'm hopeful that I get the idea across. Writing and chanting spells in Latin is not a requirement, mind you, but I like it just the same. It has an old, witchy feel to it that I like. I'm including some Latin words and phrases that I've found useful over the years. Apologies if I leave out accents, or get the conjugation wrong, etc. There are a myriad of books to have on hand for reference and I encourage everyone to learn a little Latin.

Spells can be involved or simple in nature. I prefer to stay as simple and direct as possible. When using rune magick, I can incorporate rune names into the chant or incantation because the names themselves have power. I can arrange simple language around the runes themselves, draw them in the air with my projective hand, wand, or athame, or onto a piece of paper, or in soil. I've also drawn bindrunes in sand as part of a spell. It really doesn't matter how you do it because it's the intention that matters.

A simple spell in Latin to raise energy and reveal truth might look like this:

Erigo navitas (raises energy)
Veritatem revelare (reveals truth)

It can be repeated as many times as necessary and a candle can be used as a focus. The rune, *Sowilo,* may be added to the beginning of *Veritatem revelare* for extra energetic punch.

When casting a circle, I like to visually build it, so I say:

Circulare (encircles)
Circumplecto (creates wall/shield)
Circumlevare (raises up all around)
Circumfero (casts the circle)

The nice part about this one is that each command can be directed at each quarter so that Elemental Guardians can be involved.

Spells don't have to be complicated or flowery unless you want to make them that way. Simple commands work just as well, even one word commands can be more than enough to send intention to the universe. The more poetic spells I write in English. But when I need something immediately, one or two words work just fine.

For example:

Reflexio reflects hostile energy back to its origin.

Deflexio deflects hostile energy away from you.

Dilatare expands something.

Celero quickens or hastens.

Aperio reveals or opens.

Sanescere heals wounds.

Celare hides something.

Impedio prevents or hinders.

Additional words and phrases I have found useful include:

Ut supra (as above)

*Ut infra (*so below)

*Beo existere (*Blessed be)

*Beo (*to bless)

Neuma (Spirit)

Divinia (divine)

Terra (Earth)

Aqua (Water)

Animus (Air)

Incendium (Fire)

Emanare (to flow out of)

Implicare (entwine, enfold, encircle)

Desistere   (desist from)

Dispelsatio (disperses magick)

Desiderium patefactum (manifested desire)

Solvere (scatter)

Nocere (to know)

Silentium   (to keep silence)

Velle (to will)

Audere (to dare)

Ere (to go)

Religare (bind)

I try to keep things simple when writing out a spell or chant. Otherwise I tend to make it too complicated. And when translating it into Latin, it's nice to use single words if possible essentially as commands. That's what we're doing anyway, commanding one thing or another, and simplifying it seems to make it more powerful.

When casting a circle, a more involved chant is below:

Casting a Circle

*Beo Existere (*Blessed Be)
*Circulare (*encircle)
*Circumplecto (*create wall/shield)
*Circumlevare (*raise up around)
*Circumfero (*cast the circle)
*Erigo Navitas (*raise energy) 4 times
*Veritas Revelat (*reveal truth)
*Salva Veritate (*with truth preserved)
*Existere Beo (*Blessed Be)

I don't always chant anything beyond *erigo navitas*, but I definitely do if I need to focus in on whatever truth is revealing itself.

Healing spells can be specific or general in nature. I like to include Elemental Guardians or influences in many of my spells, healing in particular.

Elemental Healing

Resonate Elementa (Elements resonate)
*Conjugant (*Combine together)
*Amoris et lux sanitas (*Bring healing love & light)
*Est conatus (*To this endeavor)
Statera te amoris (Balance, love & light for thee)
et lucis
*Voluntate servavit (*My will preserved)
*Dea bona est (*Goddess blessings to be)

Communication can be problematic from time to time and
it helps to bring everything into alignment and begin with
a positive framework.

Positive Communication

Incipere in statera (Begin in balance)

Incitare commutationem (Catalyze the exchange)

Invocare divinam (Invoke divinity within)

particulam magni

Sine libero corde (Open hearts without)

Spiritus infundere (Infuse Spirit into will)

In voluntatem

In voluntate autem mea (My will into being)

Next is an example of simplified language in a spell for alignment.

Alignment

Spiritus dilatere (Expand Spirit)

Creare statera (Create balance)

Mutatio invocet (Invoke change)

Emanare (Flow)

Tranquillavit (Restore tranquility)

It's easy to see how simple commands can be most effective. Next is a more complicated protection spell.

Protection

Custodes elementis (Elemental Guardians)

Nunc audite vocem meam (Hear my voice now)

Quaeram Dea protection (I seek Goddess Protection)

Et hoc votem (And this I vow)

Et ligabis ea hominem *(I bind this person)*

Nocere non (To harm none)

Et Illuminare quod (And awaken as)

cogitations una (thoughts become one)

My goal in any spell, particularly when seeking to change another's behavior is for the individual to awaken to his/her Source within. This binding spell gives the person a time out to reassess and see the folly of their behavior.

The next spell is another command-oriented spell, again with the focus on healing and alignment. Unwanted behavior doesn't come from Source, but from ego. All that's truly needed is awakening to that fact.

Stop Unwanted Behavior

Veritas revelat (Reveal truth)

Oblonquuntur moribus (Interrupt behavior)

Removet claustra (Removes barriers)

Coalescit (Coalesces)

*En statera (*In balance)

I've often wondered when doing a binding spell, who exactly am I binding? Since I create all that I see and experience, then am I really influencing another's behavior, or am I only influencing my own view of the situation? And do I have the right to influence another's behavior? How do I know that what's happening isn't exactly what that person needed at the time? Maybe I'm only a player in his or her experience. Why would I try to affect that in any way? It's one thing to keep myself safe, but to do anything beyond that may reflect judgment on my part.

There's a certain honor involved in the life of a witch. Casting this or that spell that causes harm or seeks retribution seems judgmental and aggressive. Do we as witches have the right to interfere in another's life experience when we have no idea what their initial intention was before incarnating into form? Sometimes the more difficult choice for the witch is to simply let someone be. Observe without becoming involved.

If we create what we see, then why are we seeing anything that makes us uncomfortable? Maybe that's the better question to ask. Perhaps the shift that's needed is in our own perceptions. It may sound like avoidance, but if we're not in full creation mode at all times, then we're becoming stuck in someone else's reality. We either remember we're Source Energy in physical form, or we become the bodies we inhabit. If our focus remains on the body level, then we find ourselves reacting to everything we see. So are we casting spells to control our own alignment with Self, or are we trying to change others? I have a feeling that as long as we cast spells for alignment, we're in a far better position than trying to change everyone around us. Anyway, it's something to consider, no matter what the witch decides.

Divination

Runes

Runes are both a language and a divination tool. Their energies are useful in rune magick, as the witch combines runes together into a meaningful sigil. That in turn may be carried, worn, drawn on a candle, or a piece of paper which can then be burned, the ashes buried, cast into water, or scattered to the wind. Even carrying a rune that resonates is a wonderful thing to do. I wear Algiz for protection and Hagalaz as a witch rune. There is an Elder Futhark, and a Younger Futhark, as well as a myriad of other runic languages.

Elder Futhark

The Elder Futhark is comprised of twenty-four runes and is said to be given to the world by Odin. I've been drawn to runic symbols since I was a young child. I had no idea of the ancestral connection, but it makes sense now. I use the Elder Futhark exclusively as it resonates more than the others, although I find them interesting as well. Below are the runes, their respective meanings, and some correspondences I've found over the years. As with all the other correspondences, they've been cobbled together from a variety of sources.

ᚠ

Fehu represents wealth, abundance, and life force. Energy is manifested with this rune and it's useful in increasing the effect of other runes.

ᚢ

Uruz is the rune of changes, of energy shaping matter, our focus into form. It represents courage and can be used to overcome obstacles, both self and other imposed.

ᚦ

Thurisaz is the hammer of Thor, representing giants and chaos. The rune of catalytic energy, Thurisaz brings new beginnings and renders opposition useless against you. It can be used in weather and love magick as well as protection and defense.

ᚨ

Ansuz is Odin's rune representing communication, wisdom, and spiritual awareness and can be used to channel the Higher Self. The rune of the Mind, Ansuz brings clarity to any situation.

ᚱ

Raidho is the journey we take while in physical form. It speaks of purpose and harmony, preferring the process to the goal. It can be used to bring balance, for astral travel and hedge riding, and alignment with Higher Self.

ᚲ

Kenaz is the torch and is considered the rune of openings. Secrets revealed, purification, and enlightenment are among the energies of Kenaz. Magickal workings with Kenaz center on clarity, intuition, and awakening.

ᚷ

Gebo is the gift, and indicates balanced energy exchange as well as partnerships of all kinds. It can be used magickally to join something or people together, for fertility, and to increase a spell's effectiveness.

ᚹ

Wunjo means joy and is regarded as the wish rune. It indicates peace, contentment, and harmony and may be used in magickal workings to attract a partner.

ᚺ

Hagalaz is Urdh, a Norn rune representing the past. It also represents hail and is considered to be the rune of the witch in that like the witch, Hagalaz causes disruption prior to eventual change. It may be worn as a talisman for protection or used in magickal workings for hedge riding, reducing a fever, preventing storms, and blessing a marriage.

ᚾ

Nauthiz represents need and a link between destiny's influences. Another Norn rune, Nauthiz represents Skuld, the Norn of the future. It assists in achieving goals and creating positive change. It's useful in love magick and binding spells as it shapes outcomes in positive ways.

ᛁ

Isa means ice or stillness. Representing Verdandi, the Norn of the static realm, Isa halts undesired situations, shields negative energy, and assists in the development of the will. Isa represents our inward focus, giving us time to center and achieve necessary clarity.

ᛃ

Jera means year and is the rune of transformation and balance. Because of its energy of fertility, Jera is useful as part of a garden bindrune as it moves energy and invokes change for the better. Jera is also useful to align relationship energy.

$$\Lambda$$

Eihwaz is the rune of paradox and the connection between opposites. It provides a link between physical and nonphysical realms and is useful in magickal workings involving banishing and protection.

$$\Upsilon$$

Perthro is the rune of chance and resembles a cup for throwing dice. It's the rune of Wyrd, the unknown, the mystery of fate decided by the Norns. In magickal workings, Perthro is useful for healing and divination.

Y

Algiz represents the Elk and protection. Another rune connecting the physical and nonphysical realms, Algiz is the rune of Higher Consciousness.

ᛋ

Sowilo represents the Sun and is another rune of Higher Self. Victory, confidence, and illumination are among Sowilo's influences. Its energy is useful in meditation and hedgeriding, and it strengthens all other workings.

↑

Tiwaz is the warrior that insures justice. It represents higher ideals, order, and promises. Competition and legal matters and a victorious outcome are influenced by Tiwaz.

ᛒ

Berkano represents the birch tree and fertility. New
beginnings, ideas coming to fruition, and motherhood are
influences of Berkano. Magickal workings involve healing,
protection, and fertility.

ᛗ

Ehwaz represents momentum and the intuitive bond.
Odin's eight-legged horse, Sleipner is represented by this
rune. Given it's travel influence, I view Ehwaz as our
Merkaba, the energy field of our nonphysical Self, and it
can be used for hedgeriding and astral travel. Regarding
the intuitive bond, Ehwaz also represents marriage and
partnership.

ᛗ

Mannaz represents humanity and the integration of body, mind, and spirit. A thought rune, Mannaz increases intelligence and influence the self in society. Magickal workings influence spiritual harmony and acquiring assistance from others.

ᚱ

Laguz means water and represents our intuition. A feminine rune, Laguz is the rune of the occult, of the strong woman who aligns to achieve clarity before acting. Laguz is the rune of allowing and moving in nonresistance around obstacles and drama and may be used in magickal workings to gather energies together. Laguz is the energy of drawing down the moon and represents our inner knowing, our clairsentience and is useful in dreamwork.

◇

Inguz is the seed, the energy of potential, our genetic inheritance. The male counterpart to the feminine energy of Berkano, Inguz awakens male fertility and is used magickally for a sudden release of energy. The focus is an inner one and is helpful for centering and grounding.

⚱

Othala represents kinship and ancestral land. It's our inheritance and the rune of sacred space, balancing order with chaos. Magickal workings may center on protection, balance, prosperity, Akashic memories, and sacred space.

⋈

Dagaz means day and represents complete enlightenment. All doors are open. All options are available. One phase is ending and other beginning. The witch stands in the middle, the in between, holding the balance, as witness, as observer. The rune of the present moment, Dagaz may used to achieve balance, clarity, and alignment.

When I originally began researching runes years ago, Othala was presented last, but somehow that never seemed right. Apparently others feel the same way because now I see other authors putting Dagaz last. Given that it represents complete enlightenment I think it's appropriate. You realize you are one with everyone else, understanding your kinship with everyone resulting in spiritual enlightenment.

One thing I don't do with runes or tarot is look at reverse meanings. Duality is implied in anything of form, so it seems redundant. Plus, if we're here to see through Source Vision, then we shouldn't see the down side of anything. Besides, there are enough cards in the suit of Swords that cover the drama side of life.

Witches Runes

Over the years with my fascination for runes, I've collected images and descriptions typically associated with Witches Runes. Sets consist of varying amounts and I've collected them all and have come up with fourteen. The pictures are of runes that I've made myself.

Sun – Dynamic and expansive, the Sun's masculine energy represents growth, happiness, strength, and clarity. Making progress toward successful outcomes along with new beginnings. A rune of Elemental Fire.

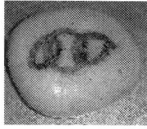

Rings - Relationships, love, and marriage, along with contractual agreements and material possessions are the influences of this rune. A rune of Elemental Water.

Flight - Awareness, awakening, and psychic ability are indicated with this rune. Additionally, unexpected news and visits are favored along with communication and air travel. An Air Element rune.

Ear of Corn - Change, progression, and unexpected news are among the influences of this rune of Elemental Earth. Fertility and growth are also influences.

Crossed Spears - arguments, opposition, frustration, stagnation, no results, challenges ahead, misunderstandings, need to make a decision

The Eye - vision, realization, awareness, clarity, transformation, psychic ability, protection.

Harvest - abundance, harvest, prosperity, money, positive growth, benefits, reap what we sow, on the right path, responsibility, don't become complacent

Man: catalytic, male figure, strength, vitality, gods,, courage, perseverance, war, chaos, action, challenge, resources, increase, instability

Moon: subtle, long-term change, feminine energy, transitions, emotions, instability, impulsive action, secret actions, magick, Esbat ritual

The Scythe: breaks curses, hexes or bad luck, dissolving a relationship, endings, danger, death, something needs ending, swift change, caution

The Star: desire, wishing, attract fortune, hopes, destiny, faith, ideals, inspiration, opportunity, unattainable love

Wave: travel by water, friendship, family, relationships, intuition, spirituality, transformation, inner essence, emotion, illusion

Woman: female figure, divine feminine, Goddess invocation, birth, fertility, nurturing, healing, Motherhood, relationships, birth of something new

Blank/Black Rune: negativity, difficulty, painful experiences, lack of alignment, center/align/know, what's hidden

Tarot

The Tarot, like runes, contain energy. The decks are varied, but their interpretations are similar. Celtic-oriented decks like *DruidCraft* are wonderful, giving me a sacred grove feel and is one of my favorite decks to use. However, *Thoth* is my all-time favorite. It's a different sort of deck and Crowley changed the order of a handful of cards as well as some names. The cards were beautifully drawn by Lady Frieda Harris, each one its own painting. The dual *Enochian Scrying/Tattva Tarot* deck is another different sort of deck with a *Golden Dawn* focus. I like using the Tattva side for daily readings. I like considering elemental influences and this deck is really informative. It's also useful as a scrying focus.

Of course the *Rider-Waite* deck is one that everyone uses, as is its *Universal* counterpart. The drawings are more clear in the Universal deck and I use that one more often than the original *Rider-Waite* deck. I also like the colorful *Morgan-Greer* deck. There are similarities between these decks, but they do reflect the perspectives of their creators. That's what I like about having various decks on hand to use. The same card is drawn in different ways, giving some insight into its creator.

Following are my impressions of the Major Arcana from the *Thoth* deck. Again, some of the names have been changed as well as their order.

Fool - at the beginning of the journey. All things are possible. Seeing with Source Vision. Taking the leap of faith into physical form

The Magus - alchemical/elemental beginnings. All resources available.

The Priestess - One with Source Energy, aligned and full of powerful intuition, her energy moves in all direction.

The Empress - regal, calm, serene, nurturing, she is Goddess as Mother as she sits between the Maiden and Crone phases of the Moon. She looks to the future with calm assuredness. Growth and fertility are among the energies of this card.

The Emperor - Fiery, catalytic presence. The Emperor looks back at the Empress, not really interested in moving forward as much as trying to get her attention perhaps. He assumes the upright position of the Hangman, as he waits for his Love. Two rams appear over his shoulders, alert and curious. The shield at his feet matches the shield at the feet of the Empress. These two are inextricably bound together.

The Hierophant - channels the Goddess, balanced energies, wisdom, grace, Higher Self

The Lovers - Blessed union, polarity, duality, both sides of an issue, celebration of union, partnership, balanced effort, commitment

The Chariot - progression, forward momentum, Kerubic images at the warrior's feet looking in all directions - unlimited options available, Abracadabra above - I create what I speak - a healing incantation, balanced energy

Adjustment - calm, rational balance, Libran energy, she controls the sword of the Magus, adjustment needed to keep balance

The Hermit - Hecate, Crone Wisdom, looking down on fertile creation, seeing through Source Vision, Source Energy lighting the way

Fortune - cycles, movement, energy moving in all directions, continued action, continued success, success achieved, more to come, balanced presence and strength

Lust - Goddess holding up the world, nurtures creation, commands elemental forces, Gaia and the force of creation

The Hanged Man - inner focus, trust, surrender, alignment with Source

𝔇𝔢𝔞𝔱𝔥 - change, rebirth, inevitability, resurrection, awareness of nonphysical aspect of self, the Grim Reaper dances as the cycle of death and rebirth continues

𝔄𝔯𝔱 - alchemical change, catalytic change, the two archer's bows appearing as two moons above with the arrow pointing upward indicate a celestial focus, Water plus Fire, transmutation, the blending of opposites or components for a higher purpose

𝔗𝔥𝔢 𝔇𝔢𝔳𝔦𝔩 - new creation or possibility awaits birth, the goat's third eye is wide open, allow Source Vision to govern choices, balanced choices, physical expression, masculine, projective energy

𝔗𝔥𝔢 𝔗𝔬𝔴𝔢𝔯 - The eye above the crumbling tower suggests seeing through Source Vision, change in preparation for something better, illusion gives way to truth, let the ego fall away, stay above the fray

The Star - movement, flow, feminine energy, emotion, intuition, emotional presence, hope, the Blessed Conduit, as above, so below, healing Source Energy

The Moon - ebb and flow, change, unknown influences, illusion gives way to clarity

The Sun - completion, energy flowing in all directions, resonance, happiness, endings and beginnings, positive outcomes

The Aeon - rebirth, ascension, Source Vision

The Universe - completion of the journey, moving back into nonphysical presence, alignment with Self

Regarding the name changes, Aleister Crowley changed Judgment to the Aeon, Temperance to Art, Justice to Adjustment, and Strength to Lust. There are many tarot books available, but at the end of the day, I like my Thoth deck because I respond intuitively to each card.

The Court cards can represent people or the characteristics of the people represented. The Princess in the Thoth deck is the Page in others, the Prince is a Knight, the Knight in Thoth is a King in most decks, and the Queen remains the Queen as she should.

Numerological meanings can be found in the next section on numerology and can be applied to the cards. Elemental energies should be considered. Wands/Rods (Fire), Swords (Air), Cups (Water), and Disks/Pentacles (Earth) are the suits and their Elemental energies.

The Minor Arcana can be viewed from the standpoint of numerology and Elemental energies. From there it's nice to look at the interpretations from other tarot readers. Various books have been written and are available from a variety of booksellers. I love other interpretations. You never know when someone will see something extraordinary that can enhance future readings. They're particularly helpful when looking at patterns and relationships between cards.

Numerology

1	2	3	4	5	6	7	8	9
A	B	C	D	E	F	G	H	I
J	K	L	M	N	O	P	Q	R
S	T	U	V	W	X	Y	Z	

Numerology is about number reduction. There are a few master numbers such as 11 and 22 that you wouldn't reduce to a single digit, but typically, that's what happens in numerology. Each number has a meaning and the meanings are remarkably prescient. As an example, let's take the word, *witch*, and find its numerical value.

Using the chart above, W=5, I=9, T=2, C=3, and H=8. Adding the numbers together, we arrive at 27. Since 27 isn't a master number, we add 2 and 7 together and arrive at 9. So, the numerological value of *witch*, is 9.

From there, we look at the numerological correspondences for the number 9 to determine its significance.

Numerological Correspondences

One – deals with new beginnings, self-development, and unity in all forms

Two – represents partnerships, expressions of duality and polarity, as well as balance

Three – embodies catalytic energy, the trinity, health, joy, creativity, Triple Goddess

Four – depicts Gaia energy, foundational and structural influences, the elements and quarters

Five – represents change and rebirth, communication, the pentagram depicting Spirit controlling matter, and challenges we face

Six – balance, integration, harmony, marriage are represented by the number six

Seven – the number of magick, seven represents divinity, intuition, psychic ability, shadow self, our will and focus

Eight – practical concerns, challenges, discipline, protection, and structure are among eight's influences

Nine – the number of completion, psychic awareness and sensitivity

So as we've already determined, _witch_ has a numerological value of nine. And from the list we see the witch is psychic, sensitive, compassionate and focused upon completion. Yep.

In a Tarot spread, it's interesting to look at the numerological value of the cards to see if a pattern emerges. See where the energy flows. And it's fine to rearrange the cards to see if a numerological pattern emerges. Never get hung up on a particular pattern from a particular spread. A predefined spread can be helpful and informative, but at the end of the day, it's _your divination_. The witch decides its significance.

Herbal Materia Medica

No hedge witch's grimoire would be complete without herbs. The final section contains my materia medica. Hedge witches are herbalists at heart and I've loved and used herbs all of my life.

Herbs are useful in magick, ritual and healing. Their magickal properties are included in the previous correspondence section. And as always, I'm not a medical professional. The information that follows is for educational purposes only and should not be viewed as recommendations for health concerns. Please see a medical professional if you have any conditions that need treatment.

Angelica - *Angelica archangelica* – Herb of the Sun **(Culpepper, 1653)**. The root is used and contains essential oils, terpenes, coumarins, miscellaneous sugars, acids, flavonoids, and sterols. Angelica is a tonic and carminative **(Barton, 1844)**. It's useful in fever, respiratory infections, digestive weakness. **(Wikipedia, Angelica archangelica, 2016)**, and as a diuretic **(Chambers, 1800)**

Decoction should be used in preparation.

Black Cohosh - *Cimicfuga racemosa* – The dried root is used. Black Cohosh acts as an emmenagogue, anti-spasmodic, anti-inflammatory, anti-rheumatic, alterative, nervine, and hypotensive. It normalizes and relaxes the reproductive system, helps painful or delayed menstruation, rheumatoid and osteoarthritis, neurological pain, and reduces menopause and perimenopause symptoms.
I include black cohosh in a menopause formula I created to treat menopause symptoms.

Decoction/Tincture

Blessed Thistle – *Cnicus benedictus* – An herb of Mars **(Culpepper, 1653)**, the roots, seeds and aerial parts are used. It has antiseptic, bitter, expectorant, tonic properties and acts as a stimulant, diaphoretic, emetic, and alterative. Typically Blessed Thistle is used as a bitter tonic **(Henkel, American Medicinal Leaves and Herbs, 1911)**, as an expectorant for respiratory conditions **(Barton, 1844)**, for fevers and stomach issues **(Henkel, Weeds Used In Medicine, 1917)**.

Infusion/Poultice

Borage - *Borago officinalis* – An herb of Jupiter, the dried leaves contain essential oils, mucilage, tannins and saponins. Borage reduces fever, purifies the blood, helps itchy skin conditions, nervousness, acts as an expectorant, anti-inflammatory, tonic, galactogogue, and diaphoretic Borage is useful as an eyewash, for adrenal stress, respiratory infections, and as a source of calcium and potassium. **(Culpepper, 1653)**

Standard Infusion/Tincture

Buchu - *Agathosma betulina* – The leaves are used and contain essential oils giving it a warm, pungent taste. It acts as a diuretic, stimulant, aromatic, carminative, and diaphoretic. An infusion is helpful for urinary conditions.

Infusion/Tincture

Burdock Root – *Arctium lappa* – An herb of Venus. **(Culpepper, 1653)** The roots, seeds, and leaves of this plant are used. The root, with its bitter constituents, acts as a liver alterative and diuretic. **(Chambers, 1800)** The seeds additionally act as a diuretic, tonic, diaphoretic, and nutritive. Burdock root is helpful with skin and urinary conditions, as a blood tonic, and with rheumatic conditions. **(Barton, 1844)**

Crushed seeds – standard infusion
Root – strong decoction

Calendula - *Calendula officinalis* – An herb of the Sun. **(Culpepper, 1653)** Calendula's flowers are used with their carotenoids, resins, and saponin constituents. It's bitter, has sterols, flavonoids, and essential oils. Calendula can be used as an astringent, anti-fungal, anti-inflammatory, and vulnerary. **(Wikipedia, Calendula officinalis, 2016)** I use it in skin creams and salves and in a martial arts bruise oil I make. It's good externally for wounds, external bleeding, bruising, strains, and burns. Internally, calendula is used for digestive issues and delayed menstruation.

Infusion/Salve/Oil/Liniment

California Poppy – *Escholtzia californiaca* – The whole, lovely plant is used in medicinal teas and formulas. California poppy, while not as sedating as its cousin the opium poppy, does have a mild sedative and anti-anxiety quality. **(Wikipedia, Eschscholzia californica, 2016)**I use it as a tea to relax in the evening or for insomnia.

Infusion/Tincture

Chamomile - *Anthemis nobilis, matricaria chamomilla, chamomilla recutita* – The delicate white flowers of the chamomile plant contain gum, resin, tannin, camphor and azulene. It acts as a tonic, mild stimulant, anodyne, stimulant, aromatic, calmative, emmenagogue, and bitter. **(Henkel, American Medicinal Leaves and Herbs, 1911)** Chamomile increases the appetite, treats digestive complaints, heals wounds, and brings emotional comfort and balance.

Standard infusion/Tincture/Salve/Lotion

Catnip – *Nepeta cataria* – The leaves and flowering tops are used medicinally containing essential oils, and tannins. Catnip's diaphoretic nature reduces fever. As a nervine, anodyne, and sedative chamomile helps with insomnia, pain, and nervousness **(Henkel, American Medicinal Leaves and Herbs, 1911) (Barton, 1844)**. The aromatic properties are good for colds and its antispasmodic properties help with spasms. It's a wonderful herb and shouldn't be reserved for a witch's familiar. Just don't tell them that.

Infusion/Tincture/Salve

Cayenne – *capsicum annuum* – The fruit is used medicinally and contains flavonoids, essential oils, vitamin A,C, and E, **(Henkel, American Medicinal Leaves and Herbs, 1911)** and capsaicin. It's helpful with respiratory complaints, infection, inflammation, in stimulating and regulating blood flow, improving cardiac strength, and digestion. **(Fernie, 1897)**

Infusion/Tincture/Poultice

Chickweed – *stellaria media* – The aerial portions of this lovely low-growing plant are used and contain bitter constituents and saponins. Chickweed is used externally for skin conditions as a poultice. Internally, chickweed is used to control weight, for respiratory conditions including fever, as a blood purifier, and for inflammation. **(Wikipedia, Stellaria media, 2016)** It combines well with other herbs.

Standard infusion/Poultice

Cleavers - *Galium aparine* – An herb of the Moon **(Culpepper, 1653)** The aerial portions of the plants are used medicinally. It's bitter and the constituents include glycosides, alkaloids, and flavonoids. **(Wikipedia, Galium aparine, 2016)** Cleavers are diuretic and are useful for fluid retention and inflammation. **(Chambers, 1800)**

Standard Infusion

Coltsfoot - *Tussilago farfara* – The leaves, roots, and flowers are used medicinally. Constituents include mucilage, and a bitter flavor **(Barton, 1844)**. Coltsfoot is used for respiratory complaints, skin disorders, infections, and rheumatic problems. **(Wikipedia, Tussilago, 2016)**

Infusion/Tincture

Comfrey - *Symphytum officinale* – The leaves and roots are medicinal and include mucilage, allantoin, alkaloids, saponins, and tannins. **(WIkipedia, 2016)** Comfrey acts as a demulcent, vulnerary, expectorant, and astringent. It's used for respiratory and gastric complaints, to regulate blood sugar, and to heal wounds and breaks.

Decoction/Tincture/Poultice
Foot Soaks – decoct, strain and add to foot soak water. I decoct roots several times, so I let the strained herb cool and then freeze it until the next time I need an herbal foot soak. Because they're that fabulous.

Cramp bark - *Viburnum opulus* – Also known as Guelder Rose, the bark is the medicinal part of the plant. It has bitter constituents along with arbutin, tannins, coumarins, catechins, and hydroquinone. As a nervine, its antispasmodic, anti-inflammatory properties make it useful for uterine and menstrual issues as well as muscle spasms. **(Wikipedia, Viburnum opulus, 2015)**

Decoction/Tincture

𝔇andǝlion - *Taraxacum officinale* – An herb of Jupiter **(Culpepper, 1653)**The whole plant is used medicinally. Dig roots in the spring and fall; harvest leaf and fresh flowers during the spring and summer months. Dandelion contains vitamins and minerals including Vitamin s A, C, E, and K, and calcium, iron, magnesium, and potassium. It also contains glycosides, terpenes, flavonoids, and is bitter. **(Wikipedia, Taraxacum officinale, 2016)** If all we had were dandelion to use for medicine, we'd be just fine. It basically covers all the bases. It's diuretic, laxative, antirheumatic, and tonic; you name it, it does it. It increases bile, and reduces fluid retention and fever. **(Barton, 1844)** It's the one herb I cannot do without.

Infusion – leaf/Decoction – roots/Tincture – both/Poultice

𝔇ong Quai - *Angelica sinensis* – The root is used medicinally and is bitter and acrid. Dong Quai acts as a uterine tonic, antispasmodic, and alterative. It treats hypertension, insomnia, and cramps, and purifies the blood. Dong Quai treats female reproductive conditions and relieves symptoms related to menopause. **(Wikipedia, Angelica sinensis, 2016)**
I include Dong Quai in a menopause formula I take daily for balance.

Standard decoction/Tincture/Capsules

𝔈chinacǝa 𝔯oot - *Echinacea augustfolia, purpurea* – The root is medicinal and contains glycosides, essential oils, volatile oils, and saccharides. Echinacea stimulates the immune system and acts as an antidepressant, among other things. It treats a variety of infections and is used externally on wounds. **(Wikipedia, Echinacea purpurea, 2016)**

Decoction/Tincture/Poultice

Elderberry - *Sambucus nigra* – The bark, leaves, flowers, and berries are medicinal and are bitter, they contain resin, acid, volatile oils, fat, chlorophyll, gum and starch. Elderberry acts as a purgative, diaphoretic, emetic, and it's helpful with respiratory conditions, particularly the flu. **(Barton, 1844)**

Standard Decoction/Tincture

Elecampane - *Inula helenium* – An herb of Mercury **(Culpepper, 1653)**, the root is used and contains inulin, volatile oils, resin, mucilage, and is bitter. Elecampane is an expectorant, tonic, and diuretic and treats respiratory infections. **(Barton, 1844)** A stomachic, elecampane also treats digestive complaints **(Chambers, 1800)**

Standard Decoction/Tincture

Fenugreek - *Trigonella fornumgraecum* – The seeds are medicinal and are bitter, carminative, and emollient, and contain mucilage, volatile and fixed oils . Fenugreek stimulates breast milk production and treats respiratory conditions and digestive complaints. **(Barton, 1844)**

Decoction/Tincture

Feverfew - *Tahaietum parthenium* – An herb of Venus **(Culpepper, 1653)**, the flowers and leaves are medicinal and are considered bitter and pungent and contain resin and mucilage as well as a blue volatile oil. Feverfew is stomachic, antispasmodic, diuretic, and a uterine stimulant. **(Chambers, 1800)** The herb stimulates menstruation and relieves gravel **(Culpepper, 1653)**

Fresh leaf/flower Infusion/Tinctur

Garlic - *Allium sativum* – Mars is its ruler **(Culpepper, 1653)**, the bulb itself is medicinal and contains essential oil and is mucilaginous. It's diaphoretic and expectorant, diuretic and antiseptic. It's also a stimulant and it stimulates digestion, heals wounds, and reduces swelling. **(Barton, 1844)**

Include in tea/Poultice

Ginger - *Zingiberis officinalis* – The root is medicinal containing volatile oils, manganese, and other vitamins and minerals. Ginger is a stimulates circulation, soothes respiratory conditions and fevers as well as indigestion. **(Wikipedia, Ginger, 2016)**

Infusion/Decoction

Ginseng - *Panax ginseng* – The root is used and is mucilaginous, aromatic and bitter. **(Hanbury, 1862)** It contains ginosides, gintonin, and phytoestrogens. An adaptogen and yin in nature, is reportedly a stimulant and aphrodisiac. **(Wikipedia, Ginseng, 2016)**

Decoction/Capsules

Goldenseal Root - *Hydrastis Canadensis* – The root is medicinal – contains alkaloids, resin and is bitter. Goldenseal is a tonic, alterative, and deobstruent.**Invalid source specified.** It's a bitter, hepatic, anti-inflammatory, antimicrobial, an emmenagogue, and a laxative used for digestive complaints and to stimulate appetite, female reproductive issues, skin problems. **(Wikipedia, Goldenseal, 2016)**

Decoction/Tincture

Hawthorn – A tree of Mars and Fae folk **(Culpepper, 1653)**, Hawthorn contains flavonoids, acids, and tannins. Hawthorn is used as a cardiac tonic and digestive. **(Wikipedia, Crataegus, 2016)**

Infusion/Decoction/Tincture

Horehound – *marubium vulgare* - An herb of Mercury **(Culpepper, 1653)**, horehound is used for cough and other respiratory ailments. **(Hill, 1812)** It's also used for worms and stomach complaints. **(Henkel, American Medicinal Leaves and Herbs, 1911)**

Infusion/Tincture/Syrup/Candy

Horsetail – *Equisetum segetale* – An herb of Saturn, the herb stops bleeding both internally and externally, is a diuretic, treats respiratory complaints. **(Culpepper, 1653)**

Infusion/Tincture

ℌops – *Humulus lupulus* – Mars is its ruler, hops has bitter and tannin properties. It's an alterative, tonic, antiseptic, stomachic, and diuretic and contains lupulin giving it a sedative quality. Hops can also be used in a poultice for rheumatic complaints and bruising. **(Fernie, 1897)**

Infusion/Tincture/Poultice

ℌyssop – *Hyssopus officinalis* – An herb of Jupiter and Cancer, hyssop soothes respiratory ailments, externally applied heals wounds. **(Culpepper, 1653)** Hyssop can also be infused for use as a compress for sore joints and muscles and bruising as well as to promote menstruation. **(Fernie, 1897)**

Infusion/Compress

Juniper – *Juniper communis* – Solar herb – the berries are diuretic in nature and carminative. **(Culpepper, 1653)** Juniper berry treats kidney stones and the crushed berries can be used as a poultice for neuralgia or rheumatic pain. **(Fernie, 1897)**

Decoction/Tincture/Poultice

Lemon Balm – *Melissa officinalis* – an herb of Jupiter and Cancer **(Culpepper, 1653)**, its constituents include tannins and volatile oil and treats respiratory ailments and digestive complaints. **(Waggaman, 1895)** Lemon balm, with its nervine properties, alleviates headaches and nervous tension. **(Fernie, 1897)**

Infusion/Tincture

Licorice – *Glycyrrhiza glabra* – With Mercury as its ruler, Licorice treats respiratory and rheumatic complaints. **(Culpepper, 1653)** The root is used medicinally and has a sweet taste. Its constituents include sugar, starch, and resin and have demulcent and expectorant properties. **(Waggaman, 1895)**

Decoction/Tincture

Marshmallow Root – *Althaea officinalis* – Venus is its ruler **(Culpepper, 1653)** and its constituents include sugar, fixed oil, mucilage and starch. Marshmallow is demulcent and soothing. **(Waggaman, 1895)** Its diuretic and emollient properties assist in the treatment of kidney stones. Externally as a poultice Marshmallow root soothes inflamed joints, swellings and bruises, and sore muscles.

Decoction/Poultice

Motherwort – *Leonjurus cardiaca* – An herb of Venus and Leo, Motherwort strengthens the heart and acts as diuretic. **(Culpepper, 1653)** It's also useful as a tonic and diaphoretic **(Henkel, American Medicinal Leaves and Herbs, 1911)** and promotes menstruation. **(Hill, 1812)** It has bitter properties as well as an alkaloid, glycosides, tannins, volatile oils, and flavonoids. **(Wikipedia, Leonarus cardiaca, 2016)**
I love motherwort. I include it in tea blends and I make a tincture which I use in tea. It's relaxing without feeling sedated.
Infusion/Tincture

Mugwort – *Artemisia vulgaris* – An herb of Venus **(Culpepper, 1653)**, Mugwort acts as an emmenagogue and narcotic bringing on menses and treating nervousness. It's useful in ritual as a smudge for astral travel, hedge riding, and divination. Mugwort can be smoked or used as a tea or part of a blend. It can also be tinctured.

Infusion/Tincture/Smudge

Mullein – *Verbascum album* – An herb of Saturn **(Culpepper, 1653)**, Mullein acts as an astringent and vulnerary as well as an expectorant and antispasmodic and its mucilaginous nature is useful for respiratory conditions including cough. **(Chambers, 1800)** The leaf is bitter and stalks are dipped and burned as hag's or witch's tapers. The leaves can be smoked for respiratory conditions. The flowers can be infused into oil to treat ear aches. **(Fernie, 1897)**
I use the flowers for their anodyne properties in bruise oil, and I tincture the root for arthritis pain and inflammation.

Infusion/Tincture/Poultice/Oil/Salve

Nettle – *Urtica diotica* – Mars governs the Nettle plant and aids respiratory conditions including asthma and hay fever. Nettle is a diuretic, expectorant, and tonic and controls inflammation and fluid retention associated with rheumatic conditions.
I include nettle in almost every tea I make. It's a little bitter so I include milder herbs along with Stevia if I have it. I also tincture nettle as a simple.
Infusion/Tincture

Oats, Oatstraw – *Avena sativa* – Oatstraw mucilaginous nature acts as a restorative and nervine and is wonderful for nervous stress and exhaustion of all types. **(Fernie, 1897)** Both the oats and the oatstraw are used medicinally, harvesting them when both are a light, milky green color. Oats contain sugars and gum as well as avenin and lignin **(Waggaman, 1895)**

I use oatstraw in so many of my infusions. I typically add it as a nutritive, but it's so relaxing that I make sure to add it to evening tea blends.

Infusion/Tincture

Parsley Root – *Petroselinium vulgare* – An herb of Mercury **(Culpepper, 1653)**, Parsley root stimulates the appetite and treats urinary conditions **(Chambers, 1800)**. It clears splenic and liver obstructions and treats cough, and as a poultice reduces bruising.

Standard Infusion/Tincture

Pennyroyal – *Pulegium vulgare* – An herb of Venus, pennyroyal treats cough and rheumatic complaints **(Culpepper, 1653)**. Pennyroyal's medicinal properties act as a carminative, stimulant, and emmenagogue, and it's used as an insect repellent. **(Henkel, American Medicinal Leaves and Herbs, 1911)**

Standard infusion/Tincture

Peppermint – *Mentha piperita* – Peppermint is cooling and pungent and contains gum, tannin, resin and volatile oil. Peppermint is a stimulant and carminative, a nervine, and is antiseptic, and is typically used in tea for digestive conditions.**Invalid source specified.** But it's also wonderful whenever you need a quick pick-me-up in lieu of caffeine.

Infusion

Pipsissewa — *Chimaphila umbellate* — Having a bitter, astringent taste, Pipsissewa's tonic and diuretic properties make it an excellent herb for rheumatic complaints. **(Henkel, American Medicinal Leaves and Herbs, 1911)**
I include pipsissewa in tincture blends for rheumatoid arthritis.

Infusion/Tincture

Plantain — *Plantago major* — An herb of Venus **(Culpepper, 1653)**, plantain is a wonderful herb to use as a poultice to heal wounds and treat insect bites. Internally, plantain treats urinary conditions, **(Chambers, 1800)** intestinal complaints, liver issues, and respiratory conditions. Pain, swelling and inflammation due to rheumatic disorders are also treated with plantain poultices **(Culpepper, 1653)**.
This is one of my all-time favorite herbs. I can walk anywhere on my property and find either this version or the slender ribwort version for any kind of insect bite I might get. I smash it up a couple of leaves and then apply it directly to bite or abrasion. In seconds, the itch of a mosquito bite goes away. I've infused it in witch hazel or rubbing alcohol for a fine liniment and include it in a refreshing summer spray I've formulated. Plantain is versatile like the dandelion. I can't do without either.

Infusion/Tincture/Liniment/Poultice

Red Clover – *Trifolium pretense* – Used in tea, red clover acts as an alterative, anti-spasmodic, expectorant, and anti-inflammatory. **(Wikipedia, Trifolium pratense, 2016)**
I use it for respiratory and menopause symptoms. I have a field of red clover that my bees simply love!

Standard infusion

Sage – *Salvia Officinalis* – An herb of Jupiter **(Culpepper, 1653)**, bitter and astringent, sage contains tannins, volatile oils, resins, and terpines. It's used as a stimulant and tonic **(Waggaman, 1895)**. Sage strengthens and calms the nerves and promotes menstruation **(Chambers, 1800)**. It also calms rheumatic pains and is used as a gargle for sore throats **(Culpepper, 1653)**.
Of course sage is wonderful as a smudge during ritual or anytime you want to purify, cleanse, or consecrate a new ritual tool, sacred space, or for smudging negative energy from your home. The dried leaves can be burned on charcoal in a cauldron or tossed into a larger fire.

Standard Infusion/Smudge

Sarsaparilla – *Smilax officinalis* – Mucilaginous, starchy, and bitter, sarsaparilla also contains acids, glucosides, and resins. It acts as a liver alterative, purifying the blood, and treats symptoms associated rheumatic conditions.**Invalid source specified.** Sarsaparilla also acts as a diuretic and diaphoretic. **(Hill, 1812)**

I use sarsaparilla in a tincture I formulated for rheumatoid arthritis.
Infusion/Tincture

𝕾𝖆𝖘𝖘𝖆𝖋𝖗𝖆𝖘 – *Sassafras* officinale - the bark is used medicinally and smells wonderful! It's pungent, bitter, aromatic, and astringent and contains gum, waz, oil, resin, and tannins **Invalid source specified.**. Sassafras acts as a diuretic, alterative, and diaphoretic **(Hill, 1812)**.
I use sassafras in the same tincture with sarsaparilla for RA.

Infusion/Tincture

𝕾𝖐𝖚𝖑𝖑𝖈𝖆𝖕 – *Scutellaria lateriflora* – a bitter herb that contains tannins, fat, sugar and a volatile oil, skullcap acts as a nervine and is used for sleep and nervous exhaustion **(Fernie, 1897)**. With its bitter principle, skullcap is also considered a tonic and also functions as an antispasmodic **(Waggaman, 1895)**.

Standard infusion/Tincture

𝕾𝖑𝖎𝖕𝖕𝖊𝖗𝖞 𝕰𝖑𝖒 – *Ulmus rubra* – the inner bark is used medicinally and has a bland, mucilaginous quality. It's demulcent and is used for inflammation **Invalid source specified.**, and as a poultice for skin conditions **(Chambers, 1800)**.

Decoction/Capsules/Poultice

$\mathfrak{Spearmint}$ — *Mentha spicata* — similar in properties to peppermint, spearmint has a milder taste and is used for digestive complaints.
I include spearmint in many tea blends to give them a fresh, minty flavor. I actually prefer it to peppermint.

Infusion

$\mathfrak{St.}$ $\mathfrak{John's}$ $\mathfrak{Wort}$ — *Hypericum peiforatum* — An herb of the Sun and Leo, St. John's Wort externally treats wounds. Internally it treats rheumatic complaints **(Culpepper, 1653)**. Noted as a *Witch's Herb*, St. John's Wort may prove helpful during exorcisms. It's diuretic, alleviates depression and respiratory complaints. **(Fernie, 1897)**
I use St. John's Wort in an oil by itself or infused with Arnica for rheumatic pain. I also use it as a tea or tincture. And clearly the next time I need an exorcism..

Infusion/Tincture/Oil/Salve

$\mathfrak{Valerian}$ $\mathfrak{Root}$ — *Valeriana officinalis* — The root is used medicinally, smells awful and tastes bitter. It has a volatile oil, tannin, mucilage, acids, resin, and starch and is considered a nervine and anodyne. It's also antispasmodic in nature **Invalid source specified.**. Valerian is useful for nervous tension and headaches **(Hill, 1812)**, and may also be useful as a laxative **(Fernie, 1897)**.
Valerian smells bad and that's a good thing. I've used it in tea blends and tinctures. Because of its volatile oil, valerian should be infused, not decocted. Steep 1 tsp root for 15 minutes away from heat. Do not boil or the volatile oil will dissipate.
Infusion/Tincture

Wild Cherry Bark – *Prunus virginiana* – A useful cough remedy, Wild Cherry Bark contains resins, tannins, acids, and is considered bitter with a tonic and sedative action **(Waggaman, 1895)**.
I use Wild Cherry Bark and Elderberry both as tinctures to support Winter health.

Tincture

Wood Betony – *Betonica officinalis* – An herb of Jupiter and Aires, Wood Betony is considered a liver alterative, effective against worms, a carminative, diuretic, and a bitter **(Culpepper, 1653)**. It treats headaches, stimulates appetite, and is helpful with rheumatic pain **(Fernie, 1897)**.

Infusion

Wormwood – *Artemisia absinthium* - An herb of Mars, Wormwood is a bitter herb that expels worms **(Culpepper, 1653)**. It contains resin, acids, starch, and tannin. It's also used in making absinthe **(Fernie, 1897)**. Wormwood is a stomachic and aids digestion, and is effective for fever **(Henkel, American Medicinal Leaves and Herbs, 1911)**.

Standard infusion

Yarrow – *Achillea millefolium* – An herb of Venus **(Culpepper, 1653)**, Yarrow is an astringent and vulnerary, and has tannin, resin, acid, and gum constituents. It also treats respiratory conditions, and treats wounds and fever **(Fernie, 1897)**.

Standard Infusion, salve

Yellow Dock Root — *Rumex crispus* — Jupiter governs Yellow Dock which is considered a liver alterative **(Culpepper, 1653)**. Astringent and bitter, Yellow Dock treats skin and liver conditions, respiratory ailments, and fever **(Henkel, Weeds Used In Medicine, 1917)**.

Because it's an alterative, Yellow Dock is useful for rheumatic conditions such as rheumatoid arthritis.

Standard Decoction/Tincture

In Conclusion

I've enjoyed putting this grimoire together. I've edited and re-edited and I've made every attempt to streamline everything into the basics that most witches I'm aware of use. From there, the witch is limited only by her imagination and creativity. At the end of the day, the power is inside each of us and that's all any of us really needs.

The reference material I used was from public domain sources and it was wonderful. I highly recommend reading it. The information on herbs from the 1600's is just as relevant today as it was then.

Magickal references were just as interesting to research. From Agrippa to King Solomon to Ptolemy, it's a fascinating window into how these people viewed witchcraft, magick, and women.

Let your grimoire serve as your reference, as a place for your thoughts as you move through life. Try to set it high enough off the floor so that confused cats don't christen it their own. The pages stick together and the smell alone is enough to toss the thing in the garbage, tears and all.

So that's it, I guess. I hope you enjoyed reading this grimoire and I hope it helps and inspires you in creating your own.

Blessed Be!

References

Agrippa vo Nettesheim, H. C. (1898). *Three Books of Occult Philosophy or Magic.* Chicago: Hahn & Whitehead.

Ashmand, J. (1822). *Ptolemy's Tetrabiblos.* London: unreadable.

Barton, B. H. (1844). *British Flora Medica or, History of the Medicinal Plants of Great Britain.* London: Henry G. Bohn, York Street, Covent Garden.

Chambers, J. M. (1800). *A Pocket Herbal.* London: P. Gedge.

Culpepper, N. (1653). *The Complete Herbal.* London: Thomas Kelly.

Fernie, W. T. (1897). *Herbal Simples Approved for Modern Uses of Cure.* Philadelphia: Boericke & Tafel.

Hanbury, D. (1862). *Notes on Chinese Materia Medica.* London: John E. Taylor.

Henkel, A. (1911). *American Medicinal Leaves and Herbs.* Washington DC: Government Printing Office.

Henkel, A. (1917). *Weeds Used In Medicine.* Washington DC: Government Printing Office.

Hill, S. J. (1812). *The Family Herbal.* London: Tiranti Ltd.

Hopkins, M. W.-F. (1647). *The Discovery of Witches.* Norfolk: Matthew Hopkins.

Levi, E. (1896). *Dogme et Rituel de la Haute Magic, Part I: The Doctrine of Transcendental Magic.* London: Rider & Company.

Nickell, J. M. (1911). *J. M. Nickell's Botanical Ready Reference.* Chicago: Murry & Nickell Mfg. Co.

Papus. (1896). *Absolute Key to Occult Science, The Tarot of the Bohemians, The Most Ancient Book in the World.* London: George Redway.

V, K. J. (1597). *Daemonologie.* unknown: Robert Waldegraue.

Waggaman, S. M. (1895). *A Compendium of Botanic Materia Medica.* Washington D.C.: W.H. Lowdermilk & Co.

Wescott, W. W. (1911). *Numbers, Their Occult Power and Mystic Virtues, 3rd Ed.* London: Theosophical Pub. Society.

Wikipedia. (2015, August 24). *Viburnum opulus.* Retrieved from Wikipedia: https://en.wikipedia.org/wiki/Viburnum_opulus

Wikipedia. (2016). *Angelica archangelica.* Wikipedia.

Wikipedia. (2016). *Angelica sinensis.* Wikipedia.

Wikipedia. (2016). *Calendula officinalis.* Wikipedia.

WIkipedia. (2016). *Comfrey.* Wikipedia.

Wikipedia. (2016, April 16). *Crataegus.* Retrieved from Wikipedia: https://en.wikipedia.org/wiki/Crataegus

Wikipedia. (2016, March 18). *Echinacea purpurea.* Retrieved from Wikipedia: https://en.wikipedia.org/wiki/Echinacea_purpurea

Wikipedia. (2016). *Eschscholzia californica.* Wikipedia.

Wikipedia. (2016, May 12). *Full Moon.* Retrieved from Wikipedia: https://en.wikipedia.org/wiki/Full_moon

Wikipedia. (2016). *Galium aparine.* Wikipedia.

Wikipedia. (2016, April 17). *Ginger.* Retrieved from Wikipedia: https://en.wikipedia.org/wiki/Ginger

Wikipedia. (2016, April 17). *Ginseng*. Retrieved from
    Wikipedia: https://en.wikipedia.org/wiki/Ginseng

Wikipedia. (2016, April 14). *Goldenseal*. Retrieved from
    Wikipedia:
    https://en.wikipedia.org/wiki/Goldenseal

Wikipedia. (2016, February 26). *Leonarus cardiaca*.
    Retrieved   from   Wikipedia:
    https://en.wikipedia.org/wiki/Leonurus_cardiaca

Wikipedia. (2016). *Stellaria media.* Wikipedia.

Wikipedia. (2016). *Taraxacum officinale.* Wikipedia.

Wikipedia. (2016, February 22). *Trifolium pratense*.
    Retrieved   from   Wikipedia:
    https://en.wikipedia.org/wiki/Trifolium_pratense

Wikipedia. (2016). *Tussilago.* Wikipedia.

About the Author

Jan Erickson is an empath and witch in her Crone years. She has a BA in Psychology, and facilitated her two sons' homeschooling efforts. Jan earned her Black Belt in Kenpo Karate in 1991, after which she taught along side her husband in their dojo. A Reiki Master and Herbalist, Jan and her husband live on the High Desert of Central Oregon, gardening and beekeeping. Be sure to follow Jan on Facebook, Twitter (Mistress_Jan), and other social media. And check out her blog, *Stepping Aside*, where you'll find all sorts of interesting things about cannabis, astrology, and all things witchy.

Made in the USA
Las Vegas, NV
29 November 2020

11684888R00087